What People Are Saying about Jerry Wiles and *No Greater Joy...*

I know of no person more qualified to write a book like *No Greater Joy* than Jerry Wiles. Sharing his faith is a lifestyle Jerry has cultivated over decades of witnessing, and it's a lifestyle that's contagious. Catch it and be a carrier! There's no greater joy.

—*Dr. Dick Eastman*
International President, Every Home for Christ

Dr. Jerry Wiles's new book, *No Greater Joy*, exceeds even his earlier books. It is simple, clear, cogent, and relevant in its approach to sharing our faith. I have known Jerry for many years and have watched him share his faith with great effectiveness. This book should be read by every follower of Jesus.

—*Dr. Ted Baehr*
Chairman, The Christian Film & Television Commission
Editor-in-Chief, *Movieguide*

If anyone is qualified to author a book about sharing the gospel, it is Jerry Wiles. He is one of the most consistent witnesses I have ever known. And the beautiful thing is that it is not contrived or forced but rather spontaneous, flowing out of his intense relationship with Christ. *No Greater Joy* is more than a how-to book. As you read it, you will find that Jerry's passion for Christ and people is contagious. Not only will you have a lot more know-how but a lot more "want to," also!

—*Jerry Rose*
President, CEO, and television host, Total Living Network
Coauthor, *Significant Living*

What you get from Jerry Wiles's writing comes not only from the heart but also from real-life experience. Having known and been with Jerry on many occasions, I have had the rare experience of seeing how the Lord has used him in various situations with people from many different walks of life. The suggestions that he offers to the reader and the methods to which he alludes are tried and true.

It has been my privilege to observe and then to use these techniques in witnessing and sharing with others. Reading the book and studying and applying his suggestions will open your life to a change that will bring you closer to the Lord and His desire for fulfillment in Him.

—*Dr. Doug Hodo*
President Emeritus, Houston Baptist University

This is a book that I would encourage every Christian to read. Jerry Wiles has communicated wonderfully some vitally important concepts that any Christian can use to share the good news of Jesus Christ with others.

Experts tell us that nearly four billion people in the world are primarily oral learners. Therefore, it is important for us to learn to tell stories that communicate simply and powerfully the biblical truths that can be used by the Holy Spirit to draw people to a personal relationship with Jesus Christ. Christians of any age can be blessed and helped by this cutting-edge book.

—*Dr. Paul Cedar*
Chairman, Mission America Coalition

Jerry Wiles shares his heart about how easy it is to witness and win others to Christ. He has used this approach for years with great results. I commend this book to you as an encouraging way to change the lives of others and your own life through Christ. The stories and questions are worth the price of the book.

—*Dr. Avery Willis*
Executive Director, International Orality Network

No Greater JOY

No Greater JOY

POWER OF SHARING YOUR FAITH THROUGH STORIES AND QUESTIONS

Jerry WILES

WHITAKER
HOUSE

No Greater Joy:
Power of Sharing Your Faith through Stories and Questions

Jerry Wiles
Living Water International
P.O. Box 35496
Houston, TX 77235-5496
E-mail: JerryWiles@water.cc or info@water.cc
Web site: www.water.cc

ISBN: 978-1-60374-242-9
Printed in the United States of America
© 2010 by Jerry Wiles

Whitaker House
1030 Hunt Valley Circle
New Kensington, PA 15068
www.whitakerhouse.com

Library of Congress Cataloging-in-Publication Data

Wiles, Jerry, 1946–
  No greater joy / Jerry Wiles.
    p. cm.
  Summary: "Through solid biblical teaching and personal illustrations from years of effective witnessing, Jerry Wiles demonstrates how to introduce people to a personal relationship with Jesus Christ by telling stories and asking questions to start spiritual conversations"—Provided by publisher.
  ISBN 978-1-60374-242-9 (trade pbk. : alk. paper) 1. Witness bearing (Christianity) I. Title.
BV4520.W486 2010
248'.5—dc22
                        2010020370

1 2 3 4 5 6 7 8 9 10 ᴑᴑ 16 15 14 13 12 11 10

Contents

Introduction: Telling the Greatest Story in the World 9

1. Divine Appointments: Recognizing the Activity of God 17

2. Who You Have within You 23

3. God's Provision within You 35

4. What Assumptions Are You Making? 49

5. Participating in God's Work 63

6. Embracing God's Call 85

7. Getting Started 97

8. Moving to the Heart of the Matter 105

9. Discerning Ministry Opportunities 115

10. Ministry of Reconciliation 127

11. Seizing the Moment 143

12. Teamwork 153

13. God's Follow-up Strategy 159

14. Storying the Good News: The "Orality" Phenomenon 167

15. Five Sample Bible Stories for Sharing the Gospel
    and Making Disciples 193

Conclusion: Going, Trusting, Expecting 223

Notes 231

About the Author 235

Introduction

TELLING THE GREATEST STORY IN THE WORLD

I greeted a man in a hotel lobby one day with a joyful smile and said, "Hello, how have you been?"

The man returned my greeting. He must have thought we had met before, because he later came over to the area where I was standing and asked, "Do I know you?" I responded by saying, "I'm not sure, but we may have a mutual friend." He said, "Who would that be?"

"The Lord Jesus Christ. Do you happen to know Him?" I asked.

It turned out that he knew about Jesus but didn't have a personal relationship with Him.

That encounter opened an opportunity that resulted in my sharing the gospel and leading the man in prayer as he expressed his faith in Christ.

We never know how the Lord might be at work in someone's life until we connect and engage with him or her.

Just greeting someone and asking a simple question is sometimes all it takes to lead to a life-changing encounter.

The Holy Spirit has prepared many people to respond to Christ, and we have the privilege to be used as instruments of His redemptive activity if we remain available to Him.

As I later reflected on my encounter with this man, I thought of the Scripture where Jesus said, *"The harvest truly is plentiful, but the laborers are few. Therefore pray the Lord of the harvest to send out laborers into His harvest"* (Matthew 9:37–38).

In relation to the man who received Christ in the hotel lobby, I wondered how many people might have prayed for him and for how long—a mother, a grandmother, a teacher?

> **THE HOLY SPIRIT IS SO CREATIVE IN THE WAYS HE CAN USE US TO INTRODUCE CHRIST TO PEOPLE.**

The Holy Spirit is so creative in the ways He can use us to introduce Christ to people and bring them into the kingdom of God.

Time and again, the Lord just shows up and does remarkable things when we faithfully tell His stories and ask Spirit-directed questions.

If you have a passion in your heart to introduce others to Christ but have struggled to make that desire a reality, you will discover how to overcome those obstacles through this book.

Jesus Christ came into the world to reveal the Father (the creator God of the universe), to redeem lost humanity, and to restore us to a relationship with God.

Jesus told His disciples in John 20:21, *"As the Father has sent Me, I also send you."* And in Luke 19:10, He said, *"For the Son of Man has come to seek and to save that which was lost."* He now lives in you and me to carry out that purpose.

Engaging People with the Greatest Story

The Scriptures teach that when we experience the spiritual new birth, we become one with Christ in a spiritual union with God. When we, as followers of Jesus, are gripped with that reality and are identified with His plan and purpose, there will be a spontaneous outworking of the indwelling Christ in our lives.

Sharing the good news of Jesus will become a natural (or, rather, *supernatural*) part of our daily walks with Him.

Demonstrating and communicating the love of Christ is the very cutting edge of our Lord's Great Commission, in which He told us to go to all the world with the gospel. Yet, today, many believers have come to view witnessing in a negative vein.

A way to overcome our negative stereotype of witnessing and evangelism is to change the way we think about it. Rather than thinking of it as a duty, think of it as serving people and sharing life in Christ. Think of yourself as a "good news reporter."

Or, perhaps better yet, consider yourself the bearer of the greatest story in the world. As you tell the stories of the Bible and the teachings of Jesus, you can be used by the Holy Spirit to engage the hearts and minds of your hearers in ways that can't be done otherwise.

Why is this the case?

There are some interesting parallels between the time of Jesus and today's world. When Jesus lived on earth, He taught people who lived in an oral society—most people did not know how to read or did not have personal access to the Scriptures and other literature, and so information was passed along through the spoken word and through memorization.

Despite the proliferation of literature and other written materials in the world over the last few centuries, the majority of the people on earth today either are not literate or—and this is a vital aspect—*prefer* to take in and express knowledge mainly by the spoken word or a visual medium rather than by the written word. They are known generally as "oral preference learners."[1] Significantly, Oralitystrategies.com states, "By some estimates, at least 70% of the world's population has no literacy or such limited reading comprehension that they could not read a Bible with understanding."[2]

What this means is that no matter what culture you live in, most people learn and retain information better through hearing stories and being asked questions than by written material alone.

The growth of oral and visual preference learners in Western nations—which are considered highly literate—is related to the predominance of television, film, radio, popular music, cell phones, and the Internet. As a literate person (you may prefer to learn through written means, since you have picked up this book), you may lament the absence of highly developed literacy skills among citizens of your nation. Yet, as followers of Christ who desire to communicate the gospel effectively, we must address the reality of the ways in which many people receive and retain information today.

Your ability to interact personally with people—telling them stories and asking them specific questions about their relationships with God—can mean the difference in reaching them for Christ. I've devoted two entire chapters (chapters 14 and 15) to the topic of oral preference learning and communication, or "orality."

Christ Is Alive and Living in You

> THE WAY YOU SEE YOURSELF IS VITALLY IMPORTANT TO THE WAY YOU EXPRESS THE LIFE OF CHRIST TO OTHERS.

The way you see or think of yourself is also vitally important to the way you relate to others and express the life of Christ to them. If you see yourself the way God sees you (the way He has described you in His Word—a new creation, complete in Christ, and an able minister of the new covenant), you will be more alert to the needs of others and more responsive to the Holy Spirit's work of redemption.

Years ago, the Lord began to expose me to a body of truth that transformed my life. Two verses that really came alive to me at that time were:

I have been crucified with Christ; it is no longer I who live, but Christ lives in me; and the life which I now live in the flesh I live by faith in the Son of God, who loved me and gave Himself for me. (Galatians 2:20)

To them God willed to make known what are the riches of the glory of this mystery among the Gentiles: which is Christ in you, the hope of glory. (Colossians 1:27)

The realization that Christ is alive and living in me was a tremendous incentive to reach out to others and to share with them how He would give them abundant life, too.

No "Great People of God"—Only a Great God

As a result, I began to seriously read and study the Scriptures and to study the lives of those whom God has used in significant ways to advance His kingdom.

I discovered a common denominator in the lives of all the people I studied: there really is no such thing as a "great man or woman of God"; there's only a great God. And He is willing to be as great as He is, in and through any man, any woman, any boy, or any girl who will let Him be who He is, in and through their humanity. Likewise, there really is no such thing as a strong Christian, only a strong Christ, and He is willing to demonstrate His power, love, and life through every child of God who will let Him. And "letting" Him is what the Bible calls faith.

> WHEN JESUS CHRIST IS FREE TO LIVE HIS LIFE THROUGH US, HE WILL TOUCH THE LIVES OF THOSE AROUND US.

When Jesus Christ is free to live His life in and through us, He will touch the lives of those around us.

I began to learn that God does not show partiality (see Acts 10:34), and that He will use any and all of us when we discover who He is, living in us, and relate to Him in such a way that releases His life through us.

"Accidentally" Coming to Christ

God is not at all interested in what we can do for Him. He is interested in what He can do *through* us.

As I discovered and experienced the reality of Christ Himself living in me and my true identity in union with Him, I started to see more people come to Christ just "accidentally" than I had ever been able to lead to Him on purpose in my own strength. That made sharing the Lord Jesus with others really exciting to me. I began to have a genuine desire and inward motivation for others to know Christ in all His fullness.

Actually, years ago, I heard this statement: "There are no accidents in the Christian life." That's an interesting thought and a debatable topic. However, that quote came to my mind a few years ago when I was involved in an automobile accident. A woman ran into the back of my car on a freeway, and I did have an amazing witness and ministry opportunity because of this incident. After the accident, the woman in the other vehicle and I moved our cars off the freeway to wait for the police. I engaged her in conversation, learned that her name was Gloria, and simply asked her what

I've asked many others over the years: "Have you been thinking more about the Lord lately?"

She said, "That's interesting that you would ask; just two weeks ago, I decided to start reading my Bible." Her answer opened up a conversation that resulted in my being able to share the Lord with her and lead her in prayer as she confessed her faith in Christ. As a result of her coming to know Jesus, and in the process of filing a police report on the accident, four police officers also received a testimony of the grace of God at work in her life.

I think a better way to convey the idea that "There are no accidents in the Christian life" might be to say, "Every accident is an opportunity to see God at work." It is amazing and encouraging how God can intervene and turn any tragic situation, accident, or difficulty into a redemptive experience. It was certainly worth the inconvenience to have a part in Gloria's coming to Jesus!

Jesus Christ is actually prepared to clothe His divine activity in our redeemed humanity. Each of us has the privilege of containing the very life of God in Christ by the presence of the Holy Spirit. In fact, the same God who lived in Jesus Christ two thousand years ago now lives in you and me.

Author and theologian A. W. Tozer wrote,

All [God] has ever done for any of His children He will do for all of His children. The difference lies not with God but with us.[3]

As I grew in my awareness of all of this and the wonder of our Lord Jesus Christ, God intensified my desire for others to know what I was discovering about Him.

I found that many people I shared with were open and receptive to the Lord. Others were turned off due to negative experiences from their pasts. Yet most, if approached in an appropriate manner, were receptive.

God Has Prepared the Hearts of Many

God has prepared the hearts of many in these days who are open to Him. Furthermore, there are probably more lost people who are prepared to respond than believers actively reaching out with the gospel.

The purpose of this book is to share with you how God has worked in my own life and the lives of others and to give you a biblical foundation for being a fruitful, victorious, productive member of the body of Christ. I also want to challenge you to be intentional about sharing with others what God has so graciously shared with you—His very life.

You do not have to share Christ in the same way I do or the way anyone else does. We are each made to be a unique, creative expression of Christ. God wants you to share from your own experience how He has worked in your life.

> **WE ARE EACH MADE TO BE A UNIQUE, CREATIVE EXPRESSION OF CHRIST.**

God honors His Word, which tells us that the good news of Jesus Christ is the power of God unto salvation. The Holy Spirit will touch and change lives through you.

I am not ashamed of the gospel of Christ, for it is the power of God to salvation for everyone who believes, for the Jew first and also for the Greek. (Romans 1:16)

For the word of God is living and powerful, and sharper than any two-edged sword, piercing even to the division of soul and spirit, and of joints and marrow, and is a discerner of the thoughts and intents of the heart. (Hebrews 4:12)

Perhaps the Lord is tugging at your heart to become more intentional about sharing Christ. God places people in each of our lives who need Him. How will you respond?

As believers in Christ, we don't need any particular gifts or calling to tell the good news to others; we simply need to obey God and trust Him for the results.

If you are eager for real joy,...I am persuaded that no joy of growing wealthy, no joy of increasing knowledge, no joy of influence over your fellow creatures, no joy of any other sort, can ever be compared with the rapture of saving a soul from death.
—Charles H. Spurgeon[4]

My prayer is that even one truth or idea from the following pages will strike a chord and prompt you to share with someone whom you might not otherwise have shared with. Or, that you might see an opportunity you would otherwise have missed.

There is no greater joy than sharing your faith in Christ with others and watching God redeem and transform lives.

————

At the end of each chapter, as well as this introduction, I have provided optional questions that you may use for personal reflection and/or group discussion. These questions are designed to help you review the material from the chapter and begin to apply it specifically in your life.

Questions for Reflection and/or Discussion

1. What does Jesus Christ desire to express through you?

2. What is the cutting edge of the Great Commission?

3. If you have a negative view of witnessing and evangelism, how can you change this?

4. How does the way you see yourself affect the way you relate to others and whether you will share the gospel with them?

5. Would you say that you are intentional about sharing the gospel? Why or why not?

—1—

DIVINE APPOINTMENTS: RECOGNIZING THE ACTIVITY OF GOD

G ood morning. Has the Lord been good to you today?"

That was my greeting to a young waiter in a lingering moment before a breakfast meeting at a hotel conference facility. I approached Walter with the thought of sharing Christ. He was warm and friendly and took a few minutes to chat. After our brief exchange, I asked him if he had come to know the Lord Jesus in a personal way. He told me that he had been raised in a religious family and had attended church as a child.

I shared with Walter briefly about God's purpose and His love, about Jesus coming into the world to pay for our sins, and that He was raised from the dead so that we can have new life.

He was open and interested, so I shared Scriptures from John's gospel and the book of Romans. I asked Walter if he had ever made a commitment of his life to Christ. He said he wasn't sure how to do that.

I explained that he didn't have to be in a church building or go through a long religious ritual, but that God was right there with us, and we could include the Lord in our conversation. I told him that he could receive Christ right then. I briefly shared with him from Romans 10:9–13 about believing, confessing, and calling on the Lord.

If you confess with your mouth the Lord Jesus and believe in your heart that God has raised Him from the dead, you will be saved. For with the heart one believes unto righteousness, and with the mouth confession is made unto salvation. For the Scripture says, "Whoever believes on Him will not be put to shame." For there is no distinction between Jew and Greek, for the same Lord over all is rich to all who call upon Him. For "whoever calls on the name of the Lord *shall be saved."*

I suggested that he call on the Lord and ask Him to come into his life. I led him in a prayer something like this: "Lord Jesus Christ, I know I need You. I believe You died for me. Have mercy upon me, a sinner, and save me. I receive You into my life and ask You to make me the kind of person You want me to be. In Jesus' name, amen."

I was scheduled to be the guest speaker that day at the breakfast meeting and had arrived early, and this is why I'd had the opportunity to have the encounter with Walter.

Later that morning, as I was speaking to the group, Walter walked into the room as I was describing my earlier conversation with him. He mistakenly thought I was introducing him to say a few words and spontaneously began sharing that he had asked Christ into his life.

It was a tremendous encouragement to the eighty or so men at the breakfast, since my topic was personal evangelism. It was also a great encouragement for me to get updates about Walter for about the next fifteen years from my friends who attended meetings frequently at that hotel and stayed in touch with him.

Walter later became the catering manager at the hotel and gained a reputation as a respected employee. He had a great ministry and witness for Christ through his professional relationships.

Nothing Mystical about Sharing the Gospel

There's nothing mystical or magical about sharing the gospel and bringing people to the Lord. It's a matter of demonstrating the love of Christ and being willing to tell others about Him.

There are two important principles in sharing your faith:

1. Know who you are in Christ and who He is in you.

2. Be willing to bring Jesus into a conversation.

Knowing your true identity in Christ can make a world of difference in how you relate to others. The truth about you is that God intends for you to be the truth about Him.

God's Word tells us that we are *complete in Christ*, we are *made righteous in Christ*, we are *new creations in Christ*, we are *ambassadors for Christ*, and we are *ministers of reconciliation*. (See Colossians 2:9–10; 2 Corinthians 5:17–21.)

When we believe what God has said in His Word and act on the fact that it is true, the Holy Spirit will make it real in our experience. Real faith is acting on the promises of God.

One of my mentors from years ago, the late Manley Beasley, used to say that faith is "acting like it is so, when it's not so, in order for it to be so, because God said it's so." (See, for example, Romans 4:16–21; Hebrews 11:1.)

Acting on the Word of God converts the truth into our experience. Therefore, you can act on the truth that God is working in you "*both to will and to do for His good pleasure*," according to Philippians 2:13. You can also act on the fact that God is faithful to do—through you—what He has called you to do, according to 1 Thessalonians 5:24.

> **ACTING ON THE WORD OF GOD CONVERTS THE TRUTH INTO OUR EXPERIENCE.**

The various ministry encounters you read about in this book are illustrations of God's activity through our humanity, not illustrations of our doing something for Him.

For example, a few years ago, I was reading a popular Christian magazine and came across an article written by a man with whom I had shared the gospel about ten years earlier. I had actually witnessed to him on a couple of different occasions before he received Christ.

As the Holy Spirit led me, I didn't approach our discussions in a traditional way. I never asked him to pray a prayer or do any of the typical things you might think to request of people when witnessing (although I do some of those things at other times). However, after I had talked with him about the gospel the second time, he sent me a note and told me that he had repented of his years of rebellion and had trusted Christ.

This man immediately began to share his faith, and a number of people came to the Lord as a result of His witness. In fact, he and I were able to team up in reaching several convicts in a prison through correspondence and sharing gospel literature.

Seeing God at work in these ways makes our walk with Him a high adventure every day!

Recognize the Activity of God in People's Lives

The more spiritual sensitivity we have and the more we see with the eyes of faith, the more readily we will recognize the activity of God in people's lives and the more fully we'll be able to cooperate with Him in "divine appointments."

Think of the implications of Christ living in you and wanting to express Himself through you on a daily basis.

Many Scriptures refer to our being in Christ and Christ in us. Just an awareness of our spiritual union with Him makes a difference in the way we relate to others. My former pastor once said, "Our main purpose should be to love people and tell them the truth." That really puts things into perspective in a nutshell. We are so prone to make things more complicated than they are or than God intended for them to be.

Be Encouraged That God Will Use You

I often tell people that I grew up with an inferiority complex, and then, when I became an adult, I discovered that it wasn't a complex at all; I was just inferior!

CHRIST HIMSELF IS PREPARED TO LIVE IN US AND COMPENSATE FOR ALL OUR WEAKNESSES.

Well, the truth of the matter is, we are all inferior when we compare ourselves with Jesus Christ.

The good news is that the Superior One, Christ Himself, is prepared to live in us and compensate for all our weaknesses. In fact, it's in our weakness that His strength is made perfect, according to 2 Corinthians 12:9.

God often chooses the most unlikely candidates to accomplish His most significant work.

For you see your calling, brethren, that not many wise according to the flesh, not many mighty, not many noble, are called. But God has chosen the foolish things of the world to put to shame the wise, and God has chosen the weak things of the world to put to shame the things which are mighty; and the base things of the world and the things which are despised God has chosen, and the things which are not, to bring to nothing the things that are, that no flesh should glory in His presence. But of Him you are in Christ Jesus, who became for us wisdom from God; and righteousness and sanctification and redemption; that, as it is written, "He who glories, let him glory in the LORD."

(1 Corinthians 1:26–31)

Be encouraged that God will use you in a wonderful way to share Christ with others. Keep in mind that He is available to you to the degree that you make yourself available to Him.

God will use you in powerful ways if you will fully yield to His lordship, receive the fullness of His life in you, and trust and obey Him.

Enjoy the journey!

Questions for Reflection and/or Discussion

1. What is a divine appointment?

2. What are two key principles in sharing your faith?

3. What does God's Word tell us about who we are in Him?

4. How does the Holy Spirit make God's Word real in our experience?

5. To what degree is God available to you for witnessing?

6. What steps can you take to be more effective in sharing Christ?

—2—

Who You Have within You

In its purest form, bringing others to Christ means putting yourself in a position for the Holy Spirit to win others through what He prompts you to say and do.

If you see sharing Christ as something that you, in your own strength and ability, are *supposed* to do, then you will always feel burdened. You'll always feel inadequate. You'll always feel pressured. You'll always feel guilty for not doing more and frustrated that you can't do enough. On the other hand, if you see sharing Christ as letting Him use you and work through you, then it will be a joy to see what He will do next with your life!

God's Instruments

Many times, we think equate witnessing with passing out tracts (pamphlets), ringing doorbells, or praying "the sinner's prayer" with someone. We think of sharing the gospel and seeking to lead others to Christ as something we are "doing" for God.

The truth is that the Lord desires to use each of us to share our faith with others. We are His instruments of righteousness. (See Romans 6:13.)

The wonderful thing about instruments is that they are tools in the hands of others. You are God's instrument to bring others to Christ. He directs and uses you. You yield. When I take a pen in my hand to write a letter, that pen becomes

> **You are God's instrument to bring others to Christ.**

an instrument subject to my will and direction. You and I are God's instruments, used by Him to write living letters of His love to this world.

This awareness of who we are in Christ and who He is in us is at the core of our ability to be useful in His kingdom work. It is not only the foundation, but also the motivation, for what we do and say.

+ If you don't know who Christ is in you, then what is it that you're offering somebody else?

+ If you don't know who you are in Christ, then how can you help others get to that point?

Who Is He? Who Are You?

Who is Christ in me?

Who am I in Christ?

Have you answered these two critically important questions in a definitive way in your own life?

Your ability to effectively share your faith is directly related to your having settled those key questions for yourself. Before you can ever share with others who Christ can be in their lives, you must have an assurance of who He is in your life and who you are in Him.

First, you must acknowledge that He does, indeed, live within you.

Second, you must acknowledge that the Lord's presence in your life makes you complete. He has equipped you by His own life indwelling your life and has given you all things that pertain to life and godliness. (See 2 Peter 1:3.)

Who is the Jesus who lives in you? What is His nature? He is righteous. All-knowing. Ever present. All-powerful. Holy. Forever victorious. Loving. Wise.

All of these things are in direct contrast to what we are in our natural state. As human beings, apart from Christ, we are unrighteous, unholy. We are powerless and rarely as loving or as wise as we desire to be. Our victories are fleeting, at best. In fact, Jesus said, *"Without Me you can do nothing"* (John 15:5).

However, as Christ indwells you with His Spirit, He endows you with His nature. You no longer need to rely on your own righteousness, your own strength, your own wisdom, and your own ability to love. You can rely on His righteousness, His strength, His wisdom, and His ability to love *through* you.

When Jesus Christ indwells you, He restores you to true humanity—humanity as He intended at creation.

You become a representative of Christ. Your very life is a witness to the indwelling power of God.

> **WHEN JESUS CHRIST INDWELLS YOU, YOUR VERY LIFE IS A WITNESS TO THE INDWELLING POWER OF GOD.**

Witnessing Is Based on Who You Are

Being a witness is, therefore, first and foremost something you *are*. Jesus' last recorded words on earth prior to His ascension back to heaven were these: *"You shall be witnesses to Me"* (Acts 1:8).

Note the word *"be."* Jesus didn't say, "You shall *do* witnessing." He said you are to *"be witnesses."*

Your witness about Jesus is only as good as your relationship with Jesus and the extent to which you allow Him, through the power of the Holy Spirit, to fill you and work through you.

You're Already a Witness If You Have Christ Living in You

If you confess Jesus Christ today as your Savior and Lord, you are His witness. You don't have to become a witness for Him. You already are one.

The question is not, "Am I a witness?"

The question is, "What kind of witness am I?"

If you don't know your true identity in Christ, you will end up trying to become what you think you need to be, rather than being what you have already become in Him.

Let me put it this way…

+ If you don't recognize that Jesus is righteousness dwelling within you, then you may spend years in frustration seeking to become more righteous. The fact is, you can't get any more righteousness than that which you already have in Jesus Christ, who dwells within you by His Spirit.

+ If you don't recognize that the author of all spiritual authority is dwelling within you, then you may find yourself attending a dozen seminars in a frantic search to have more spiritual authority. The fact is, you can't get any more spiritual authority than that of Jesus Christ, whose Spirit resides within you.

+ If you don't recognize that the source of all divine love is dwelling within you, then you are likely to become exhausted in your human efforts to be more loving. The fact is, all the love you could ever hope to have to share with others is already resident in Jesus Christ, who lives in you.

Many of us judge our salvation and righteousness by some kind of man-made, external standard of certain behaviors and qualifications. Forgiveness, however, isn't something you earn or display. Forgiven is what you are when you have received the Lord Jesus into your life. Righteousness, it follows, isn't something you earn. Righteous is what you are when you are forgiven by God.

Don't evaluate your ability or your qualifications to witness based on any type of skills you feel you have or don't have. View yourself as God sees you: a forgiven, righteous, fully alive representative of His Son. Jesus said, *"Do not judge according to appearance, but judge with righteous judgment"* (John 7:24).

GOD SEES YOU AS A CAPABLE WITNESS TO THE GOSPEL AND THE LIFE-CHANGING POWER OF JESUS CHRIST.

In other words, you aren't to judge according to an outer, man-created standard, but you are to see things the way God sees things. God sees you as forgiven by His Son and, therefore, fully qualified to be a witness to His Son. He sees you as a capable witness to the gospel and the life-changing power of Jesus Christ. You are an able minister of the new covenant. (See 2 Corinthians 3:6 KJV.)

Therefore, don't look at your deficiencies or weaknesses. Look at His strengths. He is the one who is flowing in and through you.

Flowing like a River

Jesus said, *"He who believes in Me, as the Scripture has said, out of his heart ["innermost being"* NASB] *will flow rivers of living water"* (John 7:38). Notice that Jesus said, *"…will flow."* We don't have to initiate or engineer the process. And yet, how many of us think that we are the ones who need to prime the inner pump or make things happen? Rivers don't need to be made to flow; they need only to be *allowed* to flow.

Stated another way, you don't need to "work up" witnessing in the same way that you might prepare a presentation, a project, or a performance. You simply need to allow Jesus within you to flow out to those around you as naturally as inhaling and exhaling.

A baby is born to breathe. It doesn't need to learn to breathe or take a course titled Oxygen Exchange 101. No, the baby opens its mouth for that first gasp of air at birth and breathes.

After you are born anew spiritually, you don't need to acquire the skill of witnessing. You simply need to let Jesus flow through you to others.

This is not to minimize or downplay the value of training and developing skills. It is to say that skills *apart* from the anointing of the Holy Spirit have little value; skills acquired and submitted to the anointing of the Holy Spirit are, on the other hand, very valuable.

I recommend education and training. I believe we should get as much as the Lord allows and leads us to get. However, sometimes we think we need more education in order to serve God and to share Christ. In reality, we can start where we are and with what we have.

Renewing His Flow

"But," you may say, "nothing seems to be flowing."

Then go back to Jesus. Don't turn to something man has created or engineered. Turn back to the Lord and trust His promise to you: *"If anyone thirsts, let him come to Me and drink. He who believes in Me, as the Scripture has*

> **IF NOTHING IS FLOWING FROM YOU, DRINK MORE OF JESUS. RENEW YOUR RELATIONSHIP WITH HIM.**

said, out of his heart ["innermost being" NASB] will flow rivers of living water" (John 7:37–38). If nothing is flowing from you, drink more of Jesus. Renew your relationship with Him. Take a look again at the cross and what it means to your life and to your everlasting future. Take a look again at who is living inside you and in whom you are living.

When you renew your relationship with the Lord, you revitalize your capacity to give Jesus to the world around you. Nothing else can suffice in the same way as your going to the Lord and saying to Him, "I want to know You better and be filled with more of Your presence."

Charles G. Trumbull, noted spiritual leader and author of *Victory in Christ*, tells a story about seeing from a distance what appeared to be a man pumping water from a well at a very rapid pace. The water was flowing virtually nonstop as the man pumped vigorously. He said to himself, "I've got to meet a man who can pump water like that."

As he got closer, he realized that the figure wasn't a man after all, only a wooden image of a man on a hinge connected to a water pipe. Furthermore, the water was flowing from an artesian well, and it wasn't the man pumping the water but the water pumping the man.

From a distance, it may appear that people are doing great things for God. In reality, it is God's activity in and through them that produces the results.

That's what it means to have the life of God flowing through us as witnesses. I tried for several long and tiring years to "pump up" enough righteousness to share with others. But when I discovered the overflowing power of the Holy Spirit working through me, it became a real joy and delight to share Christ with others, and I began to see real fruit from my witness.

Part of that fruit is that when someone comes to faith in Christ, there is often a ripple effect as others come to the Lord through the new believer's testimony.

For example, one of our neighbors came to Christ through a Bible study we hosted in our home. As a result, over the next few months, his sister (who was an alcoholic) and his brother-in-law also received the Lord.

You may or may not receive feedback on or be aware of all the Lord does through one person who comes into a vital relationship with the living Christ through your witness. Yet it's encouraging to observe the reproducing life of Jesus Christ as the seed of His Word takes root in individuals' hearts.

Majid was a service station attendant where I often stopped to buy gas. After we'd had a few casual conversations, I asked him about his interest in spiritual matters and his relationship with the Lord.

He told me that, ten years earlier, a businessman from another state had been traveling through town and had given him a Bible. After he'd had the Bible for about a year, he'd started reading it somewhat but didn't understand it.

I took that as my cue to share with him the main message of the Bible and how God's plan of salvation was fulfilled in Jesus. Majid eagerly embraced the gospel and confessed his faith in Christ.

After a number of follow-up visits to the gas station and spending time with Majid, I found out that no one else had ever spoken to him about Jesus in the fifteen years that he had been in the United States.

I kept in touch with him, and he attended church with me on one occasion, which was the first time he had ever been in a church.

A few months after Majid had received Christ, I learned that he had led the owner of the gas station to the Lord. Some time later, the owner's wife said to him, "Whatever you did for my husband, can you do it for my son, also?"

I subsequently learned that Majid had led his sister and additional family members to receive Christ as he talked with them by telephone in his home country in the Middle East.

He became very active in sharing his faith, and over the next year or so, many of his other family members, friends, and coworkers came to faith in Christ through his witness.

It is amazing to see how God will use those who have little knowledge of the Bible or theology but have a basic understanding of the person and work of Jesus to boldly share Him with others.

Flowing to Overflowing

THE EARLY CHURCH WAS SO FULL OF CHRIST THAT WHAT WAS INSIDE THEM OVERFLOWED INTO EVERY CONVERSATION.

I believe the early church was so full of Christ and so full of the Spirit—Jesus' followers had believed and received so much—that their hearts were literally bubbling over with the Lord. They had such a flow of joy and peace and inner reality of the presence of Christ that they could not contain it. What was inside them overflowed into every conversation. Their conversations led to their actions. As a result, their witness was a powerful one, and the Scriptures tell us that *"the Lord added to their number daily those who were being saved"* (Acts 2:47 NIV).

For many of us, "confessing" the Lord—active, ongoing witnessing about Him—is difficult because we simply aren't believing the right things about Jesus or because we aren't receiving enough of the Holy Spirit's provision into our lives that we are filled to overflowing!

He who believes in Me, as the Scripture has said, out of his heart will flow rivers of living water. (John 7:38)

Out of the abundance of the heart the mouth speaks. (Matthew 12:34)

Want flowing rivers of testimony? Believe for them! Open your life to the Holy Spirit who gives them! Want a mouth that is speaking and confessing Christ in an abundant way? Have a heart that is bursting with belief and filled to overflowing with the Holy Spirit.

If Jesus Christ is truly real to you—if He is alive and bursting forth with His power, peace, love, and joy in your life—you will *want* to share Him with others. In fact, you'll find that you can't help but speak about Him and praise Him for the good things in your life. The Lord Himself taught,

A good man out of the good treasure of the heart brings forth good things, and an evil man out of the evil treasure brings forth evil things. (Matthew 12:35)

You Are an Ambassador of the King of Kings

"We are ambassadors for Christ" (2 Corinthians 5:20). That statement isn't just a positional or judicial truth. It's an actual truth—one that lives itself out in very practical ways as you begin to live and apply what you know is true, according to God's Word. You are an ambassador of Christ, whether you believe it or not. Believing and acting on that truth makes it real in your personal experience.

> *For if the firstfruit is holy, the lump is also holy; and if the root is holy, so are the branches.* (Romans 11:16)

You are holy because you are a branch joined with Jesus, the true Vine. As Jesus said,

> *I am the true vine....You are already clean because of the word which I have spoken to you. Abide in Me, and I in you. As the branch cannot bear fruit of itself, unless it abides in the vine, neither can you, unless you abide in Me. I am the vine, you are the branches. He who abides in Me, and I in him, bears much fruit; for without Me you can do nothing....If you abide in Me, and My words abide in you, you will ask what you desire, and it shall be done for you. By this My Father is glorified, that you bear much fruit; so you will be My disciples.* (John 15:1, 3–5, 7–8)

No branch separated from its vine can survive for very long, much less produce new fruit. The same holds true for any plant separated from its roots. It will wither and die, and all of its fruit-producing potential will die with it. (We have a vivid example of that principle every Christmas season, don't we, when we see by early January how dead and brittle our cut "evergreen" branches and trees have become?)

When you abide in Jesus as a branch abides in a vine, you literally expect His life to flow into you and through you. You can accept that you are becoming more like Him every day—taking on His nature as you grow in grace and in knowledge of Him, being ever transformed into His likeness. That's the only way you can fulfill what Jesus said in the Sermon on the Mount:

> *Therefore you shall be perfect, just as your Father in heaven is perfect.* (Matthew 5:48)

"*Perfect*" in this passage means "whole" or "complete." The only way you can become complete is to allow Jesus to flow in you. You can't achieve wholeness. You can simply trust the only whole Person who ever lived to indwell you by His Spirit and to make you realize more of your wholeness day by day.

Will it happen? The New Testament declares,

He who has begun a good work in you will complete it until the day of Jesus Christ. (Philippians 1:6)

Jesus isn't going to give up on you. Count on it! Believe it! Trust God to do what He has said He will do.

You may not be all you should be today, but if you're walking in the Spirit, you're on your way to becoming more like Christ.

> YOU'RE *BECOMING* WHO GOD HAS SAID YOU *ARE*; NOW, BELIEVE AND ACT IN FAITH ON GOD'S WORD.

You may not be the best witness for Christ Jesus today, but you are His witness, and you're becoming an even more powerful and effective witness.

You may not know everything you'd like to know about Jesus or the gospel or how to share Christ, but you're learning and growing. You're *becoming* who He has said you *are*; now, believe and act in faith on God's Word.

You Don't Earn Righteousness; You Are Made Righteous in Christ

In Proverbs 11:30, we read these great words: "*He who wins souls is wise.*"

Over the years, many of us have heard that phrase in conjunction with various "evangelism drives." However, the first part of that verse is often overlooked. The full verse reads:

The fruit of the righteous is a tree of life, and he who wins souls is wise. (Proverbs 11:30)

Who are "*the righteous*"? Jesus Christ has made righteous all those who have believed in Him and accepted the sacrifice of His life as the only sacrifice necessary for the remission of their sins. If you have been born anew spiritually, you are *"the righteous"*!

Righteousness is not something you come up with, engineer, or produce in yourself. That's self-righteousness, and the Bible refers to it as being like *"filthy rags"* (Isaiah 64:6). True righteousness is that which comes from Jesus Christ. It works from the inside out. As Philemon 6 says, *"I pray that you may be active in sharing your faith, so that you will have a full understanding of every good thing we have in Christ"* (NIV).

We must each ask ourselves the question, "What is it in me that is good?"

The only truly good thing in us *is* Christ Jesus! Apart from Christ Jesus, there's nothing good in us, said the apostle Paul: *"For I know that in me (that is, in my flesh) nothing good dwells"* (Romans 7:18).

However, if you are a true child of God, Christ is in you, and you are in Him. Therefore, all of His goodness is in you. You can acknowledge and confess that goodness is part of who you are now as a follower of the Lord Jesus.

You may say, "But I don't always act very righteous. Sometimes, I do things I know I shouldn't." Your mistakes, too, are beside the point. The reality of what you are on the inside will manifest itself in time as the Holy Spirit transforms you from within and old patterns of behavior begin to slough off you like dead skin cells do. You are being remade from the inside out.

Our culture is one that says, "I'll believe it when I see it." God's way of doing things, on the other hand, is such that believing results in seeing. Believe first, and then see the results of your belief. *"Now faith is the substance of things hoped for, the evidence of things not seen"* (Hebrews 11:1).

If you look for righteousness on the outside and expect your outward behavior to result in right standing with God, you'll search forever and never find it.

However, if you believe that righteous is what you are on the inside, righteousness based on faith will begin to manifest itself on the outside.

Righteousness simply doesn't seep from your actions into your spirit. It is a reality inside your spirit that is demonstrated in your behavior as you accept your own righteousness in Christ by faith. Righteousness moves from the inside out, not from the outside in.

How does all this relate to sharing Christ?

Very directly!

> WHEN YOU BELIEVE THAT YOU HAVE BEEN MADE RIGHTEOUS, THEN YOU ACT IN NEW AND CREATIVE WAYS.

When you believe that you have been made righteous, then you act in new and creative ways.

What freedom you have! Your old self has been crucified and buried with Christ. You have been raised up with Him in newness of life and are walking a new path with Him. He calls you to righteousness. He promises to perfect you. You continue to walk in His path, however; not in your own strength, but in His. (See Romans 6:4–11.)

Questions for Reflection and/or Discussion

1. Discuss your part and God's part in leading others to Christ.

2. Briefly describe who you are in Christ, and who Christ is in you.

3. How important is having the assurance of your salvation? Why?

4. What are some significant questions to ask about the person of Christ?

5. What happens when we don't know our true identity in Christ?

6. What does living water symbolize in John's gospel?

7. What is the source of true righteousness?

8. How does the mind-set that says "I'll believe it when I see it" contrast with God's way of doing things?

—3—

GOD'S PROVISION WITHIN YOU

The crucial issue is to live in Christ Jesus—in the glory and power of God—so that everything you say and do is a reflection of who He is. That, in turn, defines who you are. It puts you in proper relationship to who He is. It fulfills why you are.

And then, you need to know what you have.

It's not enough just to know the purpose of God for your life if you don't know the *provision* that God has made for you to fulfill that purpose. Assume for a moment that your purpose is to climb to the top of a very high mountain. Knowing your purpose isn't enough. You also need to know what provision will be made for you to have what you need to undertake the trek—provision for food, water, warmth, emergencies, proper gear and clothing, and so forth.

Salvation is not just forgiveness of sins and a secure pass to live in heaven someday. Yet, for many people, that's all salvation means. I felt that way for many years.

Salvation involves so much more! Salvation doesn't only deal with the past and decide the long-range future. It provides for the here-and-now of our lives. Otherwise, we would each face a long dry spell in the desert of defeat from our salvation day to our death day—struggling in despair, with our only hope and consolation being that things aren't as bad as they once were and aren't as good as they were someday going to be.

If we view salvation that way, we'll miss the present tense of our salvation experience. All we'll have is a past experience and a hope for the future.

Let's consider for a moment just what our salvation means to us daily, at this moment.

What we have now is Christ's life in us. If Jesus is *alive* in you, that means He's moving, doing, acting...*now*!

Follow God's Leading and Trust Him

I grew up in Arkansas, and after I finished high school, I enlisted in the Air Force. I spent most of my four-year term of military service overseas. Actually, I traveled to some thirty countries during those years of service, and I returned to the States in 1968 feeling that I had seen everything the world had to offer. And yet, I had restlessness in my heart; I knew that something was missing from my life.

I had grown up in a pastor's home. I had been exposed to the gospel and knew intellectually who Jesus was. In fact, I joined the church and was baptized at the age of twelve. However, that was not enough. I didn't really have a personal relationship with the Lord Jesus. As a twenty-two-year-old who had traveled the world, I felt an emptiness in my life and finally came to realize my need to repent of my sins and trust Christ to save me. I received Christ into my life and was born again.

For the next five years, I worked hard at being a good Christian and doing good things. I was deeply committed to the Lord, and my labor for Him was sincere. But I was a defeated Christian. I was trying to live for the Lord rather than letting Him live through me.

After those five years, I had seen very little fruit from all my religious efforts. I was nearly burned out on church activities. I had struggled and strived to live a "good life" and to do what I thought was required of me, and I was ready for a change.

In desperation, I cried out to the Lord, "I give up. If You have a better way, I'm ready to receive it."

The Lord spoke to my heart, "Thanks. I've been waiting all this time for you to discover that. Now I can do something with your life."

He showed me clearly that I didn't have to do the work in my own strength. He would do the work through me. He'd prepare people. He'd show me where to go. He'd lead me in what to say. He'd do the convicting. And He'd do the saving. All I had to do was follow His lead and trust and obey Him.

> GOD WILL DO THE SAVING. ALL WE HAVE TO DO IS FOLLOW HIS LEAD AND TRUST AND OBEY HIM.

As I wrote in the Introduction, when I began to trust Him to pave the way, prepare my heart, orchestrate the encounters and the conversations, I began to see more people come to Christ seemingly "accidentally" than I'd ever been able to by trying to do it all on my own!

I am thankful for Christian parents and the spiritual heritage of my family. However, each of us must personally choose to embrace Christ and internalize the truth in our lives; it's not something someone else can do for us.

The Gift of Evangelism

Some people say to me, "Well, certain people are just born with an inherent ability to share their faith or with the gift of evangelism."

While I believe some are especially gifted in the areas of sharing Christ and leading others to faith in Him, all of us who are in Christ have the capacity to be used in these areas. And, certainly, we are all to be witnesses of Christ.

No matter how polished, strong, or capable some people seem, we all must admit someday that we have no power or authority to give ourselves another breath, another second, or another idea. We must confess, "*I can't.*"

The good news is that when you admit you can't, God steps in and says, "I never said you could. But I always said I can, and I will!"

You can't save yourself. He never said you could. He always said He would if you would simply receive Him.

You can't transform your own life into the image of Christ. He never said you could. But He can, and He always said He would if you would trust Him to lead you, guide you, and change you.

You can't change another person's life. He never said you could. He can, and He always said He would if you would plant a seed of the gospel.

Seeking to Be a Witness? Seek Christ

Again, first seek Christ. Invite Him into your life. And then you no longer need to seek what He already is within you!

I hope you will let that truth sink deep into your spirit today. If you do, it will liberate you from a great deal of striving to become something that you already are. Simply allow Jesus Christ to do His work in and through you.

I encourage you today: *Stop searching for a greater ability to witness and start releasing the nature of Christ that is already indwelling you!*

Being His witness means letting Him be and do, through you.

Keep in mind that we do not have the ability to convict people of sin, reveal Christ, or produce repentance and faith in them. Only the Holy Spirit can do that. However, we can pray, we can let Christ live in us, and we can tell others about Him.

Stop Striving and Start Releasing

The very premise for you to be a witness to Jesus Christ is for you to allow Him to do His work in you and to manifest His nature through you. If you refuse to do these things, you'll run in circles until you're ragged trying to get good enough to witness about the Lord. You'll always think there's more you should *have* or *know* before you begin to *give* the gospel to others. And the result will be that you never give.

Most followers of Christ are aware that they should witness and share their faith. Some phrase it in this way: "I know I should be doing more for the Lord," or "I know I should witness more."

When you come to know that your witness is what you are, and that what you are is based entirely on who He is within you—and, equally important, what you allow Him to be within you—then you can be free from that frustration!

I once led a series of training sessions called "Sharing our Faith" at a particular church, during which I emphasized the points we've just been discussing. A man from another local church, who had a strong desire to be more effective in personal evangelism, heard about it and attended the series.

After a few of the sessions, he became more intentional about sharing the gospel. He talked about the Lord with his customers, neighbors, family, friends, and others.

Several months after the training sessions, I reconnected with this man. He was bubbling with joy and excitement and told me that since we had last had contact, he had led sixteen people to faith in Christ. In addition, he had led his mother to the Lord over the phone just the week before.

He is an example of what can happen when we stop striving (in our own strength) and begin tapping in to the power of God and see His life released through us.

This man truly benefited from the training he received in sharing his faith, yet you don't have to take a course in evangelism before you say something to someone about the Lord.

You don't need to memorize a hundred Scriptures or recite a sequence of steps or principles or learn a new presentation technique before you bring up the name of Jesus in a conversation.

In fact, you don't even need to read the rest of this book before you witness about Jesus Christ (although I hope you will read this entire book for encouragement and instruction). You can put this book down right now and bring people to the Lord simply by telling them what you know of Jesus, who dwells within you by His Spirit, and by allowing Him to work through you.

> YOU CAN BRING PEOPLE TO THE LORD SIMPLY BY TELLING THEM WHAT YOU KNOW OF JESUS, WHO DWELLS WITHIN YOU BY HIS SPIRIT, AND BY ALLOWING HIM TO WORK THROUGH YOU.

If you have the living Christ in you, then you already have everything you'll ever need to be a witness of Him. When you have Him, you have all you need to effectively share your faith.

Again, it's a matter of acknowledging that you have the living Christ dwelling within you and then putting yourself in a position to allow Him to operate through you.

No Right Way—Only a Right Relationship

There's no right way to witness about the Lord. There's only a right relationship to have with Him—and once you have the right relationship, you have all the prerequisites you need for witnessing and sharing His life with others.

Read what the apostle Paul wrote to the Corinthians: *"For He made Him who knew no sin to be sin for us, that we might become the righteousness of God in Him"* (2 Corinthians 5:21). Christ has become your righteousness and, therefore, because He dwells in you, *you* are the righteousness of God. You don't have to go out and try to become something you already are.

Jesus' Entire Nature Is Available to You

In 1 Corinthians 6:17, the apostle Paul stated simply, *"He who is joined to the Lord is one spirit with Him."* In other words, if you confess that Jesus Christ is your Savior and Lord, you have His Spirit. You are joined with Him. You share one Spirit. The result is that all He is—His entire nature—is available to you.

The good news is that you don't have to get "good" in order to get God. Each one of us who has been reborn knows that. We know that while we were sinners, Christ died for us. (See Romans 5:8.) He saved us from our sins when we acknowledged that we were sinners, repented, and placed our faith and trust in Christ. None of us became good enough to be rewarded with salvation. We were shown the mercy of God through our believing in Jesus Christ and accepting His shed blood as the sacrifice for our sins.

> YOU RECEIVED THE LORD JESUS INTO YOUR LIFE BY FAITH. YOU ARE HIS WITNESS THE SAME WAY—BY FAITH.

The same principle holds true for witnessing. If you have Christ, you are one in Spirit with Him, and you have everything you need to be His witness. He operates in you and through you, according to His mercy and His grace, when you allow Him to operate by faith.

You received the Lord Jesus into your life by faith.

You release Him to the world—which is another way of saying that you are His witness—the same way, by faith.

Let me emphasize again that Bible reading, Bible study, prayer, and training are all very important. But many people think they are unable to witness until they know enough to answer all the questions that might come up in a witnessing encounter. The truth is, you can begin to share Christ where you are, with what you know. Trust God to work through you.

A Matter of Faith, Not Skill

All it takes to be a witness is to choose to live by faith in Christ. In other words, we must choose to put our trust in Him rather than in our own abilities and to entrust the consequences of our actions to Him.

This truth is tremendously liberating for those who would like to be effective witnesses but feel inadequate.

You took a step of faith in receiving Jesus. You believed that when you confessed your sins, repented of them, received Jesus Christ into your life, and trusted Him to fill you with the Holy Spirit, He would do it! You had faith that Jesus would be faithful to the promises in the Bible and that He would do what He said He would do on your behalf. Even today, you believe that you have eternal life. You believe your sins are forgiven. How do you believe it? By faith.

Likewise, it takes a step of faith to witness. You must believe that when you speak the truth of God, give a word about Jesus, or share a message about the gospel, God will do what He said He would do—His Word will accomplish the purposes of God for which He sends it. (See Isaiah 55:11.) We must:

- Believe that what God has said, He will do.

- Believe that what God has promised, He will fulfill.

- Believe that what God has declared to be true is true.

- Believe that what God says about you, you are.

- Believe that what God calls you to do, He means for you to do by His grace and enabling.

Faith—All Along the Way

We must truly understand that, just as it takes faith in Christ to become a child of God, it takes an ongoing faith in Him to be a fruitful and productive member of the body of Christ. Just as Christ does the saving, so He does the maintaining and the growing within you.

- You believe. He enters.

- You receive. He manifests.

- You confess who He is with your mouth. He transforms you into His likeness.

You'll find that principle of faith again and again in the New Testament. Believing, receiving, and confessing are what you do. When you believe God—no matter what—He enters the situation to do His work. When you receive His Holy Spirit's leading and provision, He begins to work in a way that readily becomes visible and recognizable. When you confess who He is, He transforms you—and often the situation or circumstances in which you find yourself—into what is pleasing to Him.

How does this relate to witnessing and sharing Christ? Before you'll ever choose to actively share your faith, you must believe that God *wants* to use you—to guide you, to work through you, to direct you, to speak through you—to save the lost. I believe that's what the apostle Paul meant when he said, *"As you have therefore received Christ Jesus the Lord, so walk in Him"* (Colossians 2:6). You receive Him, and He indwells you in order to work through you to bring others to Himself.

Furthermore, in order to effectively share your faith, you must depend upon the Holy Spirit and acknowledge the fact that He dwells within you. You must acknowledge His presence and let Him control your life. Say to Him, "Lead me. Guide me. Use me. Direct me. Speak through me. Make Yourself known to others through my life." Receiving is active, not passive. The Holy Spirit does not force Himself on you. You must trust the indwelling Holy Spirit to work through you.

How God Wants to Use You and Me

You may say, "Well, if this is God's work, why does He need me?"

It has always been God's desire to express Himself and to reveal Himself to and through His people. That's the story of the Bible. In the Old Testament, we see that God desired to show His character through Israel, His chosen people. He still desires to express who He is, and He now does so under the new covenant through those who have received His Son Jesus and acknowledge Him as their Lord.

It is God's divine and sovereign plan to reveal Himself in and through the lives of human beings.

It's a great mystery *why* God would choose this method of proclaiming His presence in the world. The fact is that this is His method, and we are invited to participate in it.

One of the greatest truths you can know about yourself is that you are destined to portray the truth about God to the world. You were designed to express His life. You cannot do what only God can do. That's a very important point. Jesus said, *"Without Me you can do nothing"* (John 15:5). On the other hand, God chooses to express Himself through people who are willing to allow Him to use them.

> ONE OF THE GREATEST TRUTHS YOU CAN KNOW ABOUT YOURSELF IS THAT YOU ARE DESTINED TO PORTRAY THE TRUTH ABOUT GOD TO THE WORLD.

Why Am I?

Many people never know their purpose in life.

In order to understand the purpose of God in your salvation, you must first begin to understand His purpose in creation. The Bible says,

> *Then God said, "Let Us make man in Our image, according to Our likeness; let them have dominion over the fish of the sea, over the birds of the air, and over the cattle, over all the earth and over every creeping thing that creeps on the earth."* (Genesis 1:26)

We read in Isaiah 43:7, *"I have created [believers] for My glory."*

You were created in God's image and likeness. You were created to have dominion over this earth. You were created to bring glory to Him.

While sin separated you from that purpose, your salvation through Jesus Christ has put you back in position to fulfill your purpose on the earth.

Romans 5:17 says, *"Those who receive abundance of grace and of the gift of righteousness will reign in life through the One, Jesus Christ."*

As I've said before, God is more interested in your *being* than He is in your *doing*.

The fact is, however, that if you are reflecting God's image and likeness to the world around you, you will be witnessing and seeking to introduce others to Christ. Those who are still in sin and desire to be free of the guilt of sin will be attracted to you as a moth is attracted to light.

If you are reflecting the glory of God, others will be drawn to Him. Your love for others, an extension of God's love for you, will be a magnet that hurting and suffering people will find irresistible.

Again, we come back to that idea of abiding in Jesus. Jesus is the only human being who completely manifested the glory of God and totally fulfilled His purpose of being in the image and likeness of God, with full dominion over the spiritual and physical realities of this world.

When Jesus is free to live His life in you, then you are in a position to be what He created you to be—a fully alive, complete human being who reflects His image and likeness to those around you. That kind of person is a spontaneous witness and will be used to bring others to Christ! People you meet will want to know what makes you different. They will be eager to discover your secret to living.

God Will Use Your Personality to Reach Others

Every person in today's business and professional world—indeed, in every segment of life—understands that there's more to an employee than a job description or an amount of productivity. Companies, as well as governments, schools, churches, and communities, are made up of *people*. Each person brings to a job description certain qualifications, traits, and abilities. Those qualities determine to a great extent the person's motivation for doing a job, his steadfastness in pursuing it to its completion, and the amount of effort, energy, and enthusiasm he will give to it.

Jesus Christ chose to indwell *your* humanity by His Spirit—to transform *you* so that through *your* life He might reveal His life to other people. In doing so, the Lord chooses to use your personality, your likes and dislikes, and your abilities, strengths, and desires as part of His method for reaching others.

> THE LORD CHOOSES TO USE YOUR PERSONALITY, ABILITIES, STRENGTHS, AND DESIRES AS PART OF HIS METHOD FOR REACHING OTHERS.

Not every person will manifest Christ in exactly the same way. There are no cookie-cutter images. God uses your creative ability to express yourself to bring others to Himself. He puts you in unique situations. He allows you to be totally and uniquely who you are as you convey Jesus Christ to the world.

Begin to see your witness of Christ as being unique to your personality. That's the way the Lord Jesus designed you.

Be who you are. Trust the Lord to personalize your witness to reflect both who you are and who He is in you.

Your Unique Style and Approach

That means, of course, that *your* style and approach to witnessing will ultimately be uniquely your own. Nobody else can do your job just the way you can do it, because nobody else has the same qualifications, talents, skills, spiritual gifts, and past experiences that you do. And, therefore, nobody else has your ideas and creative approaches. Furthermore, nobody else has the same set of motivations, the same desires, or the same personal goals and sense of purpose that you do.

Don't expect to witness and share Christ in the same way that someone else does. Do expect God to use you in a unique way to witness to those He puts in your path.

Sharing Christ involves a blending of who you are with who Christ is to reach an individual who is at a particular point on his journey through life.

Even if you choose to use somebody else's ideas and plans as a springboard, you'll eventually find yourself wanting to make adjustments here and there to accommodate who you are. That's okay! Your best approach to, or method of, sharing the Lord is ultimately the one that God tailor-makes for you.

You came to Christ in a unique way. Nobody else came to know Him in exactly the same way you did. By that, I mean that nobody else had the same set of experiences and input that you had in coming to the point where you were ready to respond to Christ, to seek forgiveness of your sins, and to be filled with the Spirit of Christ.

Nobody else heard just those worship songs or hymns, had just those conversations, or responded just the way you did. That holds true even if you were one of thousands who went forward at a Billy Graham crusade or a similar evangelistic event. Each person who walked those aisles had a unique background that led him to get up out of his chair from wherever he was sitting in the stadium and make his way down to stand and pray a sinner's prayer on the twenty-yard line.

Therefore, don't presume that every person you meet or with whom you share the gospel will respond in exactly the same way.

Realizing our need for salvation is not a matter of "one formula fits all." It's a unique process for each person because each individual has a unique pattern of sin in his life, a sense of guilt that is related to a unique set of sinful behaviors, and a unique point at which that guilt becomes so burdensome that the message of salvation is not only accepted but is eagerly desired.

In the Flow of Your Unique Life

It is in the flow of your unique life and personality that the Lord will bring people across your path so that you can share Him in your unique way. Very specifically, anticipate these things:

+ The people you encounter will be those within the normal, everyday routine of your life. You usually won't have to go out of your way to meet them—although the Holy Spirit may prompt you to do so from time to time.

+ The people you encounter will often be those with whom you can readily establish a common interest or experience.

This holds true even if you are talking with a neighbor, custodian, hotel housekeeper, taxi driver, coworker, or friend. They will be people with whom you can find an appropriate opening line of conversation.

+ The people you encounter who are open to the Lord Jesus will be those with whom you can readily establish rapport and understanding. Directing the conversation toward Christ will be natural for you. It will be thoroughly suited to the context of your life, their lives, and the work of Christ in the world.

Time and again, we read in the New Testament that Jesus encountered people *"as He went."* (See, for example, Mark 10:46–52; Luke 17:11–19.) Some of your most fruitful gospel-sharing encounters are going to come "as you go."

Although the Lord may occasionally lead you to seek out someone, most of your opportunities to share Christ with others will be right before you as you live out your life. You generally won't have to seek out opportunities. Your part, rather, is to...

> MOST OF YOUR OPPORTUNITIES TO SHARE CHRIST WILL BE RIGHT BEFORE YOU AS YOU LIVE OUT YOUR LIFE.

+ recognize the opportunities as they come.
+ speak the name of Jesus and inquire about the person's spiritual interest.
+ trust the Holy Spirit to give you just the right words.

Everything else is the work of the Holy Spirit. He is the one who transforms people and gives them new life in Christ.

The joy of joys and the wonder of wonders is that the Lord invites us to be a part of the process. He wants us to have this degree of intimate, intense fellowship with Him. He longs for us to be part of His redemptive and kingdom-building activities in the world today. He invites us along for the greatest blessing we can ever know apart from our spiritual conversions.

Such an invitation! Such a privilege! How is it that so many of us fail to RSVP?

Questions for Reflection and/or Discussion

1. What do you need in order to share Christ?

2. What is the right way to witness about the Lord? Why?

3. When is the best time for someone to begin sharing his or her faith?

4. If witnessing is God's work, why does He need us?

5. Explain the following: "Not every person will manifest Christ in exactly the same way. There are no cookie-cutter images."

6. How can you tell if a person is open to the gospel?

7. What is *your* best approach to, or method of, sharing Christ?

— 4 —

WHAT ASSUMPTIONS
ARE YOU MAKING?

According to the U.S. Center for World Mission, more than 2 billion people in the world are unreached and therefore have "no access to the Gospel."[1]

Of all the Christian pastors, evangelists, and missionaries in the world, there are still too few to accomplish the task of evangelizing the world. That's why it is so important that every member of the body of Christ be involved in spreading the good news of Jesus.

We can all be involved personally in God's redemptive activity in the world.

We can pray for and support others who are reaching the unreached. But there also are practical ways each of us can personally be involved in touching others with the gospel of Christ.

As we approach people on an individual basis, we need to avoid making various assumptions about those who don't know the Lord. Let me share what I perceive several of these assumptions to be.

Don't Assume Everyone Has Heard

In the United States, it's easy to assume that people know the full and accurate truth about Jesus. An assumption that people *don't* know about Him would be more accurate. In spite of the abundance of churches in our communities, the number of Bibles sold each year, and the number of gospel radio and television programs being aired, many, many people—some of whom are highly educated—don't have a personal relationship with Jesus.

Most people in our culture today, however, have heard the name of Jesus. Through television, radio, reading a tract, or attending church, most people know that a man named Jesus lived and that He has something to do with Christianity.

Many of the people you encounter will have some degree of false information about Jesus. In my conversations with both churched and unchurched people, I've found that people frequently have more *incorrect* information about Jesus than they have correct information. Rather than try to undo the false information that people have, put your emphasis on the *correct* information they need to have.

True, they might have heard about a baby born in a manger at Christmas. They might even know about a man named Jesus who lived on the earth two thousand years ago. They might consider Him to have been a good teacher or a highly moral person. They might know about the death of Jesus by Roman crucifixion on Good Friday. They might even know that Easter Sunday is a celebration of the fact that Jesus rose from the dead.

Yet, they may not know that the baby Jesus who was born in a manger was born to die. They may not know that the words Jesus spoke then are life-giving to their souls today. They may not know that Jesus was more than just a good person; He was the sacrifice for their sins—He paid the price of death so that they don't have to be separated from God and can live with God for all eternity. They may not know that Jesus is the only way, the only truth, the only means to eternal life.

> UNLESS PEOPLE HEAR THE LIFE-CHANGING NEWS ABOUT JESUS CHRIST, THEY CAN'T BELIEVE IN HIM AND RECEIVE HIM INTO THEIR LIVES.

Unless they hear this life-changing good news, they can't believe in Him and receive Him into their lives.

Even those who tacitly and culturally call themselves "Christians" may not know the reality of John 3:16—that *"God so loved the world that He gave His only begotten Son, that whoever believes in Him should not perish but have everlasting life."*

This, then, is the message that we must be prepared to share.

Don't Assume Somebody Else Will Do It

The Gospel Is a One-Tells-One-Tells-One Equation

The gospel message was never intended to be limited in its proclamation to an exclusive few within the church. From the very beginning, the gospel was spread by one person telling another person, that person telling yet another, and that person sharing with another, as well.

Souls are added to the kingdom one at a time. Decisions are made on an individual basis.

As I began to allow the Lord to work through me and became bolder in sharing His life within me with those around me, the Lord convinced me of something that I believe is true for all believers: *It is the Lord's desire to reproduce what He is doing in your life in the lives of literally hundreds of other people.*

Don't Leave It to "Professional" Evangelists

Don't leave it up to a radio preacher.

Don't leave it up to a television evangelist.

Don't leave it up to the missionaries.

Don't leave it up to a preacher who is holding a crusade, seminar, or meeting in your city or church.

Don't leave it up to anybody but the person who looks back at you in the mirror.

A few years ago, I had the privilege of attending an international convention of Christian leaders in our nation's capital. Thousands of Christians converged in that hotel conference center during a five-day period.

I began to ask several of the hotel workers, one by one, if they knew what the conference was all about. Several of them knew the topic of the conference and that Christian leaders were attending. Then, I asked, "Has anyone talked with you about the Lord this week?" Nearly every person I asked said no.

I took that as my cue to share the gospel with the person and to give him an opportunity to receive the Lord. "You know," I'd close, "this conference may have been designed by the Lord just for you, so that you and I would have this opportunity to meet and talk about the Lord, and so that you could have the privilege of becoming a new person in Christ Jesus today, right now." A number of people with whom I shared the gospel did receive Christ: a housekeeper, a hotel maintenance worker, a young security guard at the entrance to the exhibition area, and eight other hotel security guards.

It was a good convention for the Lord's kingdom, quite apart from the scheduled program!

One man, already a believer in Christ, told me that he had worked during the same convention for the past four years, and I was the first person to inquire about his relationship with the Lord.

I found that utterly amazing. Here were thousands of men and women supposedly convening to discuss ways in which to more effectively and efficiently spread the gospel, and they had overlooked the very people God had put in their paths. They were so busy talking to one another that they had forgotten to mention the name of the Lord to those who cleaned their rooms, carried their bags, waited on them at restaurants, called their cabs, or provided them with other normal hotel and restaurant services.

Never assume that someone else in your church, at your convention, in your Bible study, in your Sunday school class, or in your particular Christian group will share the Lord with a person in your midst. Instead, assume that sharing Christ is as much your responsibility as it is that of anyone else.

Don't Leave It to Your Pastor

THE GREAT COMMISSION OF OUR LORD CALLS EVERY FOLLOWER OF JESUS TO BE A WITNESS AND TO SHARE THE GOOD NEWS OF CHRIST.

Many Christians leave it up to their pastors or other members of their church staff to share the gospel. They believe either that it's a preacher's job to reach the unreached or that the ordained clergy are the only ones qualified for the role.

However, it's the Great Commission of our Lord to *every* follower of Jesus to be a witness and to share the good news of Christ with those who are lost.

Your pastor won't cross paths with the same people you will. Most pastors spend virtually all of their time in direct ministry to people within the church—visiting the sick, calling on the homebound, counseling those in crisis, conducting weddings and funerals, and dealing with the administrative chores involved with running a church facility—not to mention the time they spend in prayer, Bible study, and sermon preparation.

The job of sharing Christ belongs to every member of His body.

A great way to enhance our witness is to invite people to our church services, concerts, or other programs where the gospel is presented. Also, we should get new believers involved in Bible studies, with prayer groups, and under the teaching of a godly pastor.

Sharing Christ is not intended to be a lone-ranger activity but a body function—a team effort of the entire church.

Don't Assume That Anyone Is Beyond the Need for Salvation

Romans 3:23 tells us, *"For all have sinned and fall short of the glory of God."* We were all born *"dead in trespasses and sins,"* according to Ephesians 2:1.

All people everywhere need Jesus. It is through Him, and Him alone, that we can have eternal life.

Sometimes, we are reluctant to share about the Lord Jesus with those whom we perceive to be good people. You know the people I mean—they go to church; they live good, moral lives; they don't break the law.

Our nature as sinners is not the result of something we do; it's the result of something we are in Adam. (See, for example, Romans 5:14; 1 Corinthians 15:22.) We're born with a bent toward sin and a self-centered nature. Have you ever noticed that nobody has to teach a child to lie? Nobody has to teach a child to cry, "Mine!" or to give an emphatic "No!" to any hint of authority. Our self-centered, unregenerate nature is part of our inherited, fallen humanity. We need to be redeemed from sin and the self-life.

We do what we do because we are what we are. That's why we need not only Christ's sacrifice for our sins, but also His very life to take the place of what we are. The Christian life is not a matter of self-improvement but Christ replacement. It is an exchanged life.

Don't Make Assumptions about Need according to Economic Status

Don't assume that a person of one particular social class or economic status is in greater need of the Lord than a person of another class or status.

The Lord confirmed this truth to me in a vivid way one day. A friend and I were walking through a park in a large city when we spotted a fellow with a beard and ragged clothes. He was hunting through a garbage can for food. We bought him a hot dog and an apple from a street vendor and gave them to him as we engaged him in conversation. He told us he had come to the city from North Carolina four years earlier to find a job, which never materialized. He had been living on the streets most of the time since then.

My friend and I shared the gospel with him, led him to the Lord, and urged him to get in touch with the Salvation Army.

I had no more contact with the man, but, a year later, I saw my friend from the Salvation Army, who told me what happened. The street man did show up at their place. He became involved with the ministry of the Salvation Army and was running one of their mission centers.

On the same day that we encountered the man in the park, my friend and I were having dinner in a swank hotel restaurant. Seated at the table next to us was a businesswoman who was attending a convention at the hotel. She had an ID tag pinned to her expensive, conservative suit, and the label above her name said "Financial Planners."

We began to converse casually with her, and she shared with us a little about her job as a financial advisor to major corporations. She was obviously affluent and savvy. Then, without our really seeking to turn the conversation in any direction, she began to relate the last time she had been in the hotel and all that had happened in the two years since. She told of a traumatic divorce that had left her on the verge of suicide and how her son had ended up in a mental hospital.

Her life on the inside was every bit as miserable as that of the man we had met earlier in the day at the park. With her, too, we prayed, and she received the Lord into her life.

Affluent or homeless—both are without hope if they don't have the Lord.

Don't Discount the Value of Any Human Life

Very often, we tend to look at a person and say, "Wow, wouldn't it be great if *that* person came to know the Lord?"

The fact is, it's great when any person comes to know the Lord.

A person may be a world-class athlete, a movie star, a business magnate, or even the leader of a nation, but if he doesn't know Jesus, he is just as lost as any sinner.

A person may be a hotel housekeeper, a cab driver, a factory worker, or a cook in a fast-food restaurant—or, he may have no job at all, perhaps even no home—yet, if he knows Jesus, he is a child of God, a joint heir with Christ Jesus, bound for heaven. God does not show partiality in regard to a person's outward accomplishments, and He is not willing that any person should be lost for all eternity. He is equally concerned about each of us, regardless of our position in life.

May we never forget that God loves all people—regardless of their cultures, races, or creeds. He sent His Son, Jesus Christ, to pay the penalty for sin for all people who will receive this free gift of salvation with a heart of faith.

> GOD LOVES ALL PEOPLE— REGARDLESS OF THEIR CULTURES, RACES, OR CREEDS.

Every person has value in God's eyes. Our value is based on the price Christ paid for us. That's why we are all VIPs in God's sight. Although some people may be more strategic in His kingdom because of their positions or influence, we should keep in mind that every person matters to God.

Don't Assume Someone Is Too Brilliant for You to Approach

A number of years ago, I had the privilege of leading a college chemistry professor to the Lord. Later, I was amazed to discover that, before our encounter, no one had ever asked him to receive the Lord. He had heard about the Lord, but he had never been asked to believe in Him or to receive Him into his life.

Not only did this man come to know Jesus, but he also later went into full-time ministry and served as a pastor.

Don't be intimidated by a person with degrees after his name. Don't be intimidated by those who seem to have it all together in their business or professional careers. Without the Lord, these people in your life may have brilliant and successful futures on earth, but they have no future—yet—in heaven.

Trust the Lord to use the words of the simple to *"confound the wise,"* as the apostle Paul taught in 1 Corinthians 1:27 (KJV). Trust the Lord to honor the *"foolishness of preaching"* (verse 21), which is proclaiming the truth about the Lord. Trust the Lord to reveal to a person the sincerity of your heart and the truth of your words, quite apart from any appraisal of external reputation, appearance, or standing.

Don't Assume Someone Is Too Powerful or Important for You to Approach

In the same manner, don't assume that someone is too powerful or important to hear the gospel. Remember the centurion who came to Jesus, asking humbly that He send only an "order" for the centurion's servant to be healed? Jesus said about this man's request that He had seen no greater faith in all of Israel! (See, for example, Luke 7:6–10.)

I once had the opportunity to share the Lord with a high-ranking military officer who occupied the seat next to me on a commercial airline flight. I found his acceptance of the Lord to be very straightforward, very much in keeping with his military background. Sometimes, those in positions of authority understand how to receive "higher orders" very simply and obediently.

Interestingly, I received a letter from that army officer two weeks later, thanking me for sharing the gospel with him.

Don't Assume the Person Whom You Often See Knows the Lord—Ask!

A few years ago, while working with a Christian college, I had several witness encounters with some of the faculty, staff, and students. One of those was with a janitor who emptied my trash can and vacuumed my office. He had worked at the college for several years.

I chatted with this man for several weeks on the evenings when I worked late. We exchanged a little general conversation each time, and then, one evening, as I was preparing to leave the office, I felt the Holy Spirit prompting me to ask this man, "Have you received the Lord Jesus into your life personally?"

He said, "No, I haven't."

I said, "You'd like to have the peace of mind that comes from knowing that your sins are forgiven and that you have a relationship with the Lord, wouldn't you?"

He said simply, "Yes, I would."

I said, "Well, today is the day of salvation for you. You can receive the Lord into your life right now!"

We prayed there in my office. He went on about his work, and I went home. As I left, I couldn't help but wonder, *How many years has this man waited for someone in this Christian institution to ask him if he'd like to receive the Lord?*

Afterward, each time I saw this man, I tried to find something encouraging to share with him. It was a delight to see him grow in his relationship with the Lord over the next few months.

Do you work for a church, Christian institution, or ministry? Don't assume that everyone who works alongside you is a true follower of Christ. Find out where your coworkers are in the Lord. There's only one way to know for sure—ask them.

A good, "nonthreatening" way I have found is to ask something like, "Tell me, how did you come to know the Lord personally?" or "How long have you known the Lord?"

Give them the benefit of knowing the Lord. Their response to your question will usually give you a good indication as to their spiritual condition.

Don't Assume the Person Is Unreachable Because He Doesn't Speak the Same Language You Do

From time to time, the Holy Spirit has prompted me to approach someone who doesn't speak English or who speaks English as a second or third language. I've found that if the Holy Spirit is truly guiding the encounter, there's usually someone nearby who will assist as an interpreter.

During the Olympics several years ago, a friend and I worked as part of an evangelism team. One afternoon, I encountered a woman who spoke no English but showed interest when I stopped to share the Lord with her and her friend. The woman with her seemed to be in a hurry. I asked, however, "Can you tell her in Spanish what I'm telling you in English?"

She agreed, and as she repeated, phrase by phrase, the simple explanation of the good news that I was giving her, I could see that both women were very receptive to the message of Christ. As it turned out, both of them trusted the Lord for salvation. After we prayed together, their faces were filled with joy. They kept saying over and over, "Gracias, gracias, gracias."

Even after we crossed the parking lot and looked back at them, they were still smiling and waving to us.

Don't Assume a Particular Medium Is Sufficient or "Right"

Sometimes, we tend to think we know the "right" way to communicate the gospel to others. Not everyone receives truth and information in the same way—or in the same way in which we do. For example, as I mentioned in the Introduction, and as we will learn more about in a later chapter, many people prefer to receive information through oral or visual means, while others prefer to receive it through the written word. It is essential for us, as much as possible, to get to know those with whom we are interacting. At times, one or two conversations are sufficient to lead someone to Christ. Other times, I have found that recommending or giving a certain book or a copy of the New Testament is what the person needs to learn and understand the truth of Christ and His salvation. Some people like a straightforward approach, as in the example of the army officer, while others like a more gradual one. I will discuss these concepts in more depth in later chapters, but we must be sensitive to both the Holy Spirit's leading and the personalities of others in regard to the ways in which we communicate the message of the gospel to them.

> BE SENSITIVE TO BOTH THE HOLY SPIRIT'S LEADING AND THE PERSONALITIES OF OTHERS WHEN YOU COMMUNICATE THE MESSAGE OF THE GOSPEL.

Don't Assume You Must Have a Special Time or Place

The knowledge that they could receive the Lord "anytime and anyplace" was great news for Lorita and Shannon.

One evening, a friend and I decided to stop in for a meal at a favorite Mexican restaurant of ours. Halfway through the meal, I asked the waitress, "Lorita, you're with the public all the time...have you noticed a hunger among people for more of God?"

She said, "Now that you mention it, I have."

My dinner companion and I shared with her about three people we had met that morning who had received Christ. As we shared what had happened, we could see her interest. Her eyes sparkled. "Has that ever happened to you, Lorita?" I asked.

"I go to church," she said.

"Yes, but have you ever made a personal decision to ask Christ into your heart? You want to do that, don't you?"

"You mean, right here?"

"You can do it right where you are."

She prayed with me, and her face glowed as she moved on to another table to wait on a customer. At that moment, Shannon, the bartender in the restaurant, walked by.

"Did you hear the good news?" I asked her.

She stopped in her tracks. "No...what?"

"Lorita just found peace with God."

"She did? What do you mean?"

"Yes, she received Christ into her heart as her personal Savior and Lord. Do you know that you can have that same peace?"

"How?"

"By asking Christ into your heart."

"When? Where?"

"Now...right here."

Her eyes grew about as big as saucers.

Through the years, I've found that many people look at me with wide-eyed awe when I tell them they can receive Jesus anyplace and at any time. They are so relieved that they don't need to be in a church building or go through some religious ritual in order to receive Jesus into their lives. It's an absolute wonderment to them that they can receive Him right where they are.

Shannon phrased her wonder in an unusual, fresh way. She said, "You mean...you mean...I don't have to go through religion?"

"That's right!"

Standing there in her red miniskirt and fishnet stockings, balancing a tray of bottles and glasses, she repeated a short prayer with us and gave us her name and address so we could send her follow-up materials.

Finally...

Don't Assume a "No" Once Is a "No" Always

Have you shared the good news of the Lord with someone who then rejected your invitation to receive Christ? Do you see that person often— or will you see him again?

Though many people are ready to receive Jesus when you first witness to them, the majority are not. What should you do? Continue to share.

Look for ways to continue to show the kindness of God and to demonstrate the love of Christ. Without nagging, hounding, quarreling, or making a scene, look for opportunities to share the Lord with that person each time you see him.

I have a friend who frequently says to her family members who haven't received Christ into their lives, "I'm still praying for you to receive all that the Lord Jesus has to give you. I still want to live in heaven with you someday."

> THE WAY YOU TREAT PEOPLE IS MORE IMPORTANT THAN WHAT YOU TELL THEM.

Remember that the way you treat people is more important than what you tell them. And what they see in your life is more important than what you say.

Questions for Reflection and/or Discussion

1. What assumptions, including those from this chapter, have you made about other people and their potential interest in hearing the good news of Christ?

2. What types of people are you most hesitant to share the gospel with? Why?

3. What have you learned from this chapter about the assumptions you have made concerning others' spiritual readiness?

4. Who will you begin to pray for and share the gospel with in light of what you've learned from this chapter?

—5—

Participating in God's Work

We are part of a culture that says, "Let's make things happen."

Our world runs according to power. Natural power. Human power. Emotional power. The power of ideas and systems.

Yet, as we have discussed, when it comes to sharing your faith with others, there's nothing you can do to *make* a person receive Christ.

Allow the Holy Spirit to Work in the Lives of Others

You can lead people to the light, but only the Holy Spirit can compel them to open their eyes.

You can speak words of truth to others, but only the Holy Spirit can open their ears and their hearts to truly hear your message.

You can pray for people who don't know Christ, but only the Holy Spirit can quicken your prayers, and He is faithful to give a witness in the hearts of those who respond to Christ. *"The Spirit Himself bears witness with our spirit that we are children of God"* (Romans 8:16).

You can give people opportunities to receive Jesus into their lives, but they must say, "Yes." And only the Lord can change their hearts.

You can lift up His name and share His gospel, but the transformation of souls is His work.

When Jesus declared on the cross, *"It is finished!"* (John 19:30), He was making the supreme statement of all time. He had done it all, paid it all, and borne it all. The result is that there's nothing we can do, in and of our own strength, to earn God's love, mercy, or forgiveness. All we can do is receive what Jesus has done and acknowledge that the price He paid on the cross for our sins is sufficient for our redemption.

Our Participation in God's Work of Salvation

You are never in a position to say, "I did it"—about your salvation, about any miracle of God, or about others coming to Christ. The Lord alone does the transforming, life-changing work.

There are, however, a few things that the Lord expects you to do, equips you to do, and waits for you to do:

+ Pray for others

+ Live a consistent, Christ-centered life

+ Give testimony of what the Lord has meant in your life

+ Share the Word of God

The Lord will not do these things for you. They are your responsibility.

Pray for Others

Commanded to Pray

First and foremost, we are commanded to pray for "laborers." The Lord Jesus said to His disciples, *"Pray the Lord of the harvest to send out laborers into His harvest"* (Luke 10:2).

THE MORE YOU PRAY FOR THE LORD TO SEND LABORERS INTO HIS FIELD, THE MORE YOU WILL BE WILLING TO BECOME ONE!

Pray today for followers of Christ to have courage and boldness in sharing with those who need the Lord. Pray that the Lord will call more and more people to become active and intentional about sharing Christ and seeking to lead others to Him. Pray for yourself, that you might be used to bring others into the kingdom.

I firmly believe that the more you pray for the Lord to send laborers into His field, the more you will be aware of the harvest, the more you will see the need for laborers, and the more you will be willing to become one!

A Burden for Lost Loved Ones

Most Christians feel a burden—a sadness, a heaviness of heart, a deep concern—for their loved ones who haven't received the Lord into their lives. You may have shared the gospel with a loved one, but that person hasn't responded...yet. What are you to do?

Continue to pray.

Make certain, however, that you continue to pray as God would have you to pray:

+ Pray in faith. Expect the person to come to the Lord. Don't focus on the fact that your loved one is lost. Anticipate the day when he will be saved. Look forward with faith to the joy and peace that will indwell your loved one when he does come to know Jesus as his personal Savior and Lord.

+ Pray with praise. Thank God for what He is doing in the life of your loved one. He *is* at work! Don't pray with a defeated attitude. Pray with joy! Your loved one may be one day closer to salvation than he was yesterday.

+ Pray asking the Holy Spirit for guidance. Simply pray, "Heavenly Father, show me how to pray. Reveal to me the specific things I need to pray for and about." Whatever comes to mind, pray about it. You may be surprised at some of the ways the Lord directs you to pray.

+ Pray against the enemy of your loved one's soul—the devil, or Satan. Pray specifically that your loved one will see the error of false doctrine, unbelief, atheistic teachings, and hatred, and that all false teachers in his life will be exposed for what they are.

+ Pray against the forces of darkness that are keeping your loved one blind to the truth and deaf to the gospel. Second

Corinthians 10:4–5 tells us, *"For the weapons of our warfare are not carnal but mighty in God for pulling down strongholds, casting down arguments and every high thing that exalts itself against the knowledge of God, bringing every thought into captivity to the obedience of Christ."*

+ Pray with persistence. Pray and continue to pray. Jesus likened our persistence in prayer to a widow who went again and again to a judge, who eventually gave her justice because of her persistence rather than his agreement with her request! (See Luke 18:2–8.)

+ Pray for righteousness and all good things to come into your loved one's life. The Holy Spirit is the giver of life. Jesus said, *"I have come that they may have life, and that they may have it more abundantly"* (John 10:10).

I once read an article in which a man suggested that we pray for our loved ones by saying, "I present [your loved one's name] to God in the name of the Lord Jesus." This, he suggested, was a means of declaring that the person was no longer in the enemy's camp but was being held by the Lord and was in the process of being claimed by Him. What a wonderful image to hold in your mind as you pray—indeed, a wonderful reminder that God is even more concerned about the salvation of your loved one than you are.

Praying for Those Whom You Have Not Yet Met

Although we all find it much more personal to pray for friends and relatives whom we know and love, we can also ask God to give us compassion for people whom we don't know, for the lost and needy of the world.

Pray first for a change in your own heart. Ask God to make you more aware of the suffering of humanity and to reveal to you the deep hurts of people whom you encounter.

Study prayer in the Scriptures. I believe you'll discover again and again these truths about prayer:

+ Prayer strengthens you as a believer. As you pray and intercede for others, spiritual boldness wells up inside you.

+ Prayer defeats the enemy in the spiritual realm that has held the person in bondage, thus preparing the way for the seed of the gospel you present to lodge deep within the person and take root. Second Corinthians 4:4 tells us that *"the god of this age has blinded* [those] *who do not believe, lest the light of the gospel of the glory of Christ, who is the image of God, should shine on them."* You can pray specifically for a person that "the god of this age" will no longer have power to blind the person's mind.

+ Prayer opens you up to the guidance of the Holy Spirit.

+ Prayer invites the Holy Spirit to work in a situation—both in your life and in the life of the person to whom you are about to speak.

Praying with a Fellow Believer

From time to time, you'll find that the person with whom you bring up the name of Jesus is, indeed, already a believer in Him. Encourage that person in the Lord. Use your time with him to build up his faith.

You will probably discover that many believers in Christ with whom you talk are hurting in some way. Some have fallen away from vital fellowship with the Lord. They frequently are eager to return to the Lord and to renew their commitment to Him, although they may be embarrassed to go forward during a church service, reluctant to talk with their pastor, or afraid for some reason that God will no longer hear their personal petition. In many cases, they are relieved that someone has opened up the issue with them and is willing to pray with them so that they might renew their fellowship with the Lord, sense His forgiveness and cleansing, and experience His presence. What a joy it is to help the backslider "slide back" toward the Lord!

Others are experiencing a problem—a struggle against the enemy—and your expression of faith and agreement in prayer bolsters their resolve to stand firm in the Lord Jesus and to take authority over the evil that is coming against them.

And others are simply tired. The devil's constant barrage of lies has worn them down. Or, the illness of others, or sickness in their own lives—whether physical, emotional, or mental—has made them weary. Your prayers with them will buoy them up and give them the strength and courage to continue to fight the good fight of faith. (See 1 Timothy 6:12.)

You can also join with fellow believers in agreement in prayer for the salvation of others. Jesus said, *"If two of you agree on earth concerning anything that they ask, it will be done for them by My Father in heaven"* (Matthew 18:19).

Prayer Is Always Appropriate

Prayer is always an appropriate response, regardless of a person's spiritual condition. Make prayer your first priority in sharing Christ with others. As you pray, you will develop a compassion for people. Your desire to see them receive the Lord will grow. Your priorities will shift toward a greater concern for spreading the gospel.

> MAKE PRAYER YOUR FIRST PRIORITY IN SHARING CHRIST WITH OTHERS.

In addition to praying, the Lord compels you to share with others your personal stories about what He has done and is doing in and through your life. The psalmist tells us to make known the righteous acts of God and to declare His wonderful works. (See, for example, Psalm 107:8.)

Praying for Wisdom

Our prayer lives are vital parts of our participation in God's work of sharing Christ with others.

Years ago, the Lord prompted me to begin praying specifically for His enabling to effectively communicate the gospel and introduce others to Jesus.

We can count on the Lord to answer our prayers if they are in harmony with His will and purpose, as revealed in His Word.

One day, the Lord seemed to quicken to my heart a word from Proverbs 13:20, which says, *"He who walks with wise men will be wise, but the companion of fools will be destroyed."*

I claimed that verse as a promise to me and began praying that the Lord would bring me across men and women with godly wisdom and allow me to spend quality time with them and learn from them.

Shortly after I began praying that prayer, the Lord did open the door for me to get acquainted with and spend time with a number of spiritually mature, godly saints. Some of them were internationally recognized leaders whose names are well-known in the Christian world. Others were little known to the world but were faithful, effective intercessors. Still others were amazingly gifted at leading others to Christ.

I learned that these believers, whom the Lord was using in extraordinary ways, were really just ordinary people who had deep, intimate relationships with the Lord, had discovered His ways, and were available to the Holy Spirit.

If you really want to effectively share your faith and lead others to Christ, ask the Lord to allow you to spend time with those whom He is using in those areas.

It certainly is true that we become like the people we spend the most time with. If you don't personally know of such people, ask the Lord to lead you to them or to bring them across your path.

Of course, the Lord can always use the books, tapes, CDs, videos, DVDs, and additional resource materials of others to impart to you their passion, heart, and spirit of sharing life in Christ with others.

Prayer and Witness

In my own life, I've noticed the relationship between my prayer life and my witness opportunities and effectiveness.

Let me encourage you to try something I have found beneficial over the years. During your quiet times of Bible reading and prayer, ask the Lord to guide you throughout the day. Ask Him specifically to lead you to those who need the Lord and who have an open heart, prepared to respond to the gospel.

Also, ask and trust the Lord to prepare your own heart and to give you sensitivity to the Holy Spirit and to other people's spiritual conditions.

In addition to praying in this way, be prepared and expectant during the day for the Lord to answer and open up those divine encounters.

> BE PREPARED AND EXPECTANT DURING THE DAY FOR THE LORD TO OPEN UP DIVINE ENCOUNTERS.

I suggest that you also carry along some gospel literature, gospels of John, or a New Testament in your pocket or purse.

God will often answer in ways you didn't expect. But the more you do this, the more you will recognize the hand of God in your activities and interactions with people.

Keep in mind that those whom you routinely see in your neighborhood, at work, or in the marketplace may be those who have been prayed for by an interceding parent, grandparent, or friend for years. You could be an answer to their prayers.

Remember that God is looking for those whom He can use to make His name known and to reveal the way of salvation to lost humanity. (See 2 Chronicles 16:9.)

Worship and Witness

I want to reemphasize the point that God is more concerned about our being in a right relationship with Him than He is about our working or witnessing for Him.

In other words, true worship precedes effective witness.

When we worship the Lord in spirit and in truth (see John 4:23–24), He will cleanse us, fill us, and transform us. He will reign over us and also release His life through us.

We need to be intentional and faithful worshippers if we expect to be effective witnesses.

Live a Consistent, Christ-Centered Life

While prayer is the first vital aspect of what God equips and expects us to do in relation to His work of salvation, the second aspect is that we need to live consistent, Christ-centered lives. As a new believer and a college student in the late 1960s and early '70s, I sold books with the Southwestern Company in the summertime. During those five years, in addition to selling, I was involved in recruiting, training, and managing salespeople. I recruited students on more than sixty college and university campuses in twelve states. A phrase I often heard among college students in those days was "a Christ-centered life." Students often asked, "Are you living a Christ-centered life?"

I haven't heard that phrase used much in recent years, but I think it's still a good question. Consider what it means to live a Christ-centered life. When we are Christ-centered—really occupied with Christ and filled with the Holy Spirit—our lives will show it. When Jesus is the most important Person in your life, you will have a desire to talk about Him and to share Him with others.

That doesn't necessarily mean that you will have a Jesus sign on your front lawn, or that you will have a bumper sticker on your car and a placard in your office. But, living a Christ-centered life means there is the possibility of the spontaneous outworking of the indwelling Christ. He will be evident to those around you because of your attitude, your lifestyle, and your words.

So, rather than focusing on techniques, skills, and training in witnessing and sharing the gospel, as important as those are, I think it is more important to focus on Jesus. When your focus is on the Lord Jesus, you'll discover the great joy of the supernatural release of His love, power, and grace through you.

Give Testimony of What the Lord Has Meant in Your Life

Third, we are to give testimony of what the Lord has meant in our lives. Can you state in clear, straightforward terms today what Jesus Christ has done for you personally?

What Is Your Testimony?

To confess the Lord Jesus means to "speak out" what you believe in your heart about Him and to tell what you know to be true about Him—*from your own experience.*

You may have a feeling in your heart about what the Lord has done for you but have never put that feeling into words. Try writing it out using just one or two pages so that you can share your testimony in a two- to three-minute time frame.

Just to organize your thoughts, you might try this outline:

1. What your life was like before you received Christ.

2. How God got your attention and made you aware of your need for Him.

3. How your life changed as a result of you placing your faith and trust in Christ to save you.

4. What God is doing in your life now. (Perhaps a recent answer to prayer or some special blessing you have experienced.)

> SHARING YOUR PERSONAL TESTIMONY AND INCORPORATING THE GOSPEL IS ONE OF THE MOST POWERFUL WITNESSES YOU CAN GIVE.

Actually, sharing your personal testimony and incorporating the gospel is one of the most powerful witnesses you can give.

Telling our own personal stories or experiences with the Lord is something we can all do, regardless of how long we've known Him or how much (or how little) we know about the Bible.

Remember that you are the world's leading expert on *you*! You know more about yourself than anyone else on earth. So, that should give you great confidence in sharing how the Lord has worked in your life.

An Ordinary Conversion Story Will Do Just Fine!

You may think, *I don't have an exciting or dynamic testimony.* That's all right; share it anyway.

A very dear friend of mine has made it his practice for many years to share the testimonies of others. That's great! God will use that, too. It's a wonderful way of communicating the gospel by telling how God has made a dramatic change in someone else's life.

So, if you think your own testimony is not dramatic enough, just tell someone else's dramatic testimony. But, in reality, any testimony will do.

We are apt to think of people who have highly dramatic or spellbinding before-and-after testimonies as being "special" in some way.

Your ability to share your faith isn't related to the drama of your testimony. You don't need to have been saved from a rough, hard-core, on-the-brink-of-disaster life in order to influence people to come to the Lord. In truth, we all were on the brink of disaster and eternal damnation as sinners before coming to the Lord, no matter what our outward behavior or circumstances were. The strength of your testimony lies in what Jesus went through for you, not on what you went through before you met Him and received Him as your Savior and Lord!

You Can't Talk Very Well about a Relationship You Don't Have

Many people mentally accept the historical Jesus, but they do not have a personal relationship with the living Christ.

After I've led someone to the Lord and prayed with him, I frequently find that he has been a member of a church for years, and yet, this is the first time he's ever felt as if he has had a personal conversation with the living Lord or trusted Him to indwell his life with His saving, life-giving power.

I understand that. I was a member of a church for many years before I came into a personal relationship with Jesus.

It's extremely difficult to introduce someone to a person you don't know! It's like my "knowing" the president of the United States. True, I know the name of the president of the United States. I know many people who know him personally. I've been in the office where he works. I've even shaken his hand. I know how he was elected and many of the duties that occupy his time. I can describe his relationship with the Senate and House of Representatives, his Cabinet, and the Supreme Court. But, if you were to ask me, "Do you personally know the president of the United States?" I'd have to say, "No, not personally."

Furthermore, if you were to ask me to introduce you to the president, I'd have to say, "I can put you in touch with someone who might be able to do that for you, but I can't introduce you to him because I don't really know him personally."

The relationship I don't have with the president of the United States is very similar to the relationship I didn't have with the Lord Jesus Christ for many years. I went to church. I could recite verses from the Bible. I knew people who did know Jesus Christ personally. But, I didn't know Him, and, therefore, I had no basis on which to introduce Him to someone else. At that time, I might have invited a person to church, just as I might have persuaded someone to vote for a presidential candidate. But I couldn't have gotten others into heaven's throne room any more than I could have gained their entrance into the Oval Office.

Perhaps that is your situation; you know about Jesus but have never really given your life to Him. Or, maybe you have doubts about your salvation. If so, let me suggest that you trust the Lord and settle the issue today.

> If you confess with your mouth the Lord Jesus and believe in your heart that God has raised Him from the dead, you will be saved. For with the heart one believes unto righteousness, and with the mouth confession is made unto salvation....For "whoever calls on the name of the LORD shall be saved." (Romans 10:9–10, 13)

Share the Word of God

Fourth, we are to share God's Word. The Bible is God's written Word. It is your foremost reference tool in sharing the gospel with others.

From cover to cover, the Bible points to Jesus. The Old Testament gives supporting evidence and background about who the Messiah is, shows the need for Him, and prophesies His coming and His work.

THE WORD OF GOD IS FOR OUR CURRENT CIRCUMSTANCES, PROBLEMS, AND NEEDS.

The New Testament confirms the Old Testament. It tells who Jesus Christ was and is— the Messiah and King of Kings—what He said, how He works, and what we as followers of Christ can do to reflect Him to others.

The Word of God is just that—the word that the Lord has spoken to us. It's for you and me. It's for today. It's for our current circumstances, problems, and needs.

Moreover, the gospel—which literally means "good news"—is just that! It is the good news that Jesus came and died for our sins so that we could be forgiven and restored to a full and right relationship with our heavenly Father. It is the good news that Jesus rose from the dead so that we might live forever. It is the good news that Jesus has sent His Holy Spirit to indwell us and to live His life through us. Whenever we talk about the Lord Jesus or share a verse of Scripture with someone, we are sharing God's Word and good news. Learning and telling Bible stories to "oral preference learners" is another important method of sharing Christ and communicating biblical truth, as you will discover more about in chapters 14 and 15.

There is power in sharing the Word of God that few of us acknowledge and none of us fully understands. The apostle Paul wrote, *"For I am not ashamed of the gospel of Christ, for it is the power of God to salvation for everyone who believes"* (Romans 1:16). The Word of God is what brings people to the point of believing and to salvation.

When you share with others about Christ, you can always preface your remarks with what you know to be true from God's Word, such as the following:

+ God's Word says that Jesus is the Way, the Truth, and the Life. (See John 14:6.)

+ God's Word says that Jesus died for your sins so that you wouldn't have to bear the punishment for them. (See, for example, Romans 5:8–9; 1 Thessalonians 5:9–10.)

+ God's Word says that Jesus was resurrected from the dead as the firstborn of all who would be resurrected. Therefore, God's Word is saying that you and I can be resurrected, too. We can have eternal life. Jesus bought that for us on the cross. (See, for example, Romans 6:4–5; Revelation 1:5–6.)

+ God's Word says that when we believe in Him, we receive eternal life. (See, for example, John 3:16.)

+ God's Word says that when we repent of our sins and immerse our lives in the Lord, He fills us with His Spirit—

and with His Spirit, we are filled with His joy and peace. (See, for example, Acts 2:38; Romans 15:13.)

+ God's Word says that when you confess Jesus Christ as Lord, you are saved from eternal death and given eternal life. (See, for example, Romans 10:9–10; 1 John 4:15.)

Yes, the most effective tool you have in sharing Christ effectively with others is the Word of God!

Hide the Word in Your Heart

> IN ORDER TO BE ABLE TO SHARE THE WORD OF GOD YOU MUST FIRST, OF COURSE, HAVE IT IN YOUR HEART TO GIVE.

In order to be able to share the Word of God with others, you must first, of course, have it in your heart to give. You must either memorize those verses that are key to communicating who Jesus is and what He did or be able to turn to them quickly in the Bible.

When Jesus encountered the two disciples on the road to Emmaus, the Scriptures say that *"beginning at Moses and all the Prophets, He expounded to them in all the Scriptures the things concerning Himself"* (Luke 24:27).

As you read your Bible, note those verses that you might use in answering the question, "Who is Jesus Christ?" Underline those passages. Read them again and again. Ponder them in your heart. Meditate on them. Discuss them with others. Come to a sure resolution in your own heart about who Jesus is.

If you are questioning who Jesus is, I recommend that you read these four books of the Bible:

+ The gospel of John
+ 1 John
+ Romans
+ Colossians

These four books focus on who Jesus is. Read and reread them until you have a witness in your heart that you really *know* Him.

Expect to Use the Word—and Expect God to Work

Hebrews 4:12 tells us,

For the word of God is living and powerful, and sharper than any two-edged sword, piercing even to the division of soul and spirit, and of joints and marrow, and is a discerner of the thoughts and intents of the heart.

It is the Word of God that cuts through every argument and every excuse and brings a person to face himself squarely, and, in so doing, to see his need for the Lord.

Frequently, as I share with people what the Lord has done in my own life, I read or quote verses such as Romans 10:9–10, which we looked at earlier in this chapter, as well as these:

Jesus said to him, "I am the way, the truth, and the life. No one comes to the Father except through Me." (John 14:6)

Nor is there salvation in any other [than Jesus], for there is no other name under heaven given among men by which we must be saved. (Acts 4:12)

God's Word is universal; it is also extremely personal.

Stay with Foundational Truths

What are the foundational truths you need to share with a person in order to bring him to Christ? The real issues are:

+ How much does *he* need to know in order to receive Christ?

+ How much do *you* need to know in order to become a fruitful witness?

Many perceive coming to Christ and living out our faith as more complicated than it really is. The apostle Paul cautioned us about moving away from *"the simplicity that is in Christ"* (2 Corinthians 11:3).

Even if we believe that coming to Christ is a relatively simple matter, others have held to the idea that we must be highly trained, skilled, and experienced before we can lead others to Christ. That belief tends to put witnessing out of the realm of spiritual pursuit and into the realm of intellectual activity.

The fact is that a person needs to know relatively little in order to receive Christ.

By the same token, as we have seen, one needs relatively few skills in order to lead others to the Lord.

I know of a man who led a dozen people to Christ during the first six months after he was converted. There are those who bring others to Christ soon after they themselves have received Christ. We have examples of this from Scripture: the woman at the well who immediately left her waterpot and went to the town to tell the people about Jesus (see John 4:5–42) and the demon-possessed Gerasene who immediately began telling how Jesus had delivered him (see Mark 5:1–20).

So, we see that it's not our educations, skills, persuasive abilities, or personalities that bring people to the Lord. It's the work of the Spirit of God touching lives as we simply make Christ known.

What Is It That a Person Really Needs to Know?

You need to know a few basic things to share the gospel with others:

- God has a purpose and plan. (See, for example, Romans 8:28; 2 Timothy 1:9.)

- All have sinned and come short of God's glory. (See Romans 3:23.)

- Christ died for our sins. (See, for example, 1 Corinthians 15:3.)

- Christ rose from the dead so that we can have new life. (See, for example, Romans 6:4; 8:11.)

- Each of us needs to be born again in order to have a relationship with Jesus Christ. (See, for example, John 3:3.)

It has been said that John Wesley, one of the founders of the Methodist movement, was once asked why he preached so much on the subject "You must be born again." His response was, "Because, 'You *must* be born again.'"

Born again was the term Jesus used when He explained to Nicodemus, a religious leader, what was necessary in order to see and enter the kingdom of God. (See John 3:1–21.)

The Centrality of the Cross

The apostle Paul—the great missionary-evangelist of the early church—said, *"We preach Christ crucified"* (1 Corinthians 1:23), and *"God forbid that I should boast except in the cross of our Lord Jesus Christ, by whom the world has been crucified to me, and I to the world"* (Galatians 6:14).

+ It's what Jesus did on the cross that makes the difference between eternal life and eternal damnation, between heaven and hell.

+ It's our place on the cross with Him that frees us from our old life of sin to enter into newness of life.

+ It's the cross that makes possible a genuinely loving, fully restored relationship with God, and also a loving, fully reciprocal relationship with another person.

+ It's the finished work of Christ on the cross that saves us from our sin and self-effort.

+ It's Christ's work on the cross that enables us to experience His grace and abundant life.

The Holy Spirit Bears Witness to the Word

As you share the Word of God and, above all, the message of the cross with a person, the Holy Spirit will bear witness to the truth in that person's heart.

As I share verses of Scripture, I frequently ask, "You know that to be true, don't you?" It's only on a rare occasion that someone says no. The Holy Spirit confirms in the heart of a person the truth and authority of what you are saying. That person may put up a wall around his heart, but he knows, nevertheless, that he has heard a true word.

This brings us back to our central theme.

> **THE HOLY SPIRIT WILL ILLUMINATE TO ANOTHER PERSON WHAT WE ARE WILLING TO SHARE.**

The Holy Spirit will illuminate to another person what we are willing to share. It's not enough to pray. It's not enough to know the Scriptures. It's not enough to have a personal testimony. It's not enough even to know what you believe about the Lord *unless* you are willing to open your mouth and share it.

Confessing Christ—actually speaking His name and sharing about Him—has no substitute.

One of the best passages for anyone to study—and even to memorize—is Isaiah 55:10–11, which declares,

For as the rain comes down, and the snow from heaven, and do not return there, but water the earth, and make it bring forth and bud, that it may give seed to the sower and bread to the eater, so shall My Word be that goes forth from My mouth; it shall not return to Me void, but it shall accomplish what I please, and it shall prosper in the thing for which I sent it.

What an encouragement that verse should be to all of us! When we speak God's Word to others, that Word can bring life. It *will* hit God's target. God will use it in His efforts to expand His own kingdom. It *will* be worthy.

Thus, we can have the full assurance that WHATEVER we say that lifts up the name of Jesus will be as good seed on this earth.

We do the watering. He does the growing. This principle is stated in yet another way in the Bible…

We Do the Lifting, and He Does the Drawing

Jesus said, *"And I, if I am lifted up from the earth, will draw all peoples to Myself"* (John 12:32).

Our job is to lift up Jesus.

His job is to draw people to Himself.

When you show kindness and demonstrate God's love to others, you are lifting up Jesus.

When you speak the name of Jesus to a person in need, you are lifting up Jesus.

When you introduce Jesus into a conversation, you are lifting up Jesus.

When you reply with the words of Jesus (which you have learned from the Bible or which He gives you to speak at that moment), you are lifting up Jesus.

Most of us will talk to people readily about the weather, the latest song we've heard or movie we've seen, sports, and hobbies.

We'll talk about the latest political or economic news, our most recent purchase, our families, our careers, our work, and other activities.

Yet none of those things is eternal. None of those topics gives a person an opportunity to know Jesus and to experience the life He has to give. None of those things can result in everlasting life for the hearer.

When we lift up Jesus, He will draw others to Himself.

The words we speak about Jesus are like welcome drops of water on the parched souls of humanity. They cause eternal seeds within to sprout and bring forth life.

Rather than talk about the weather, let's rain on somebody's parched soul today by sharing God's Word.

It Only Takes a Spark

It only takes a spark to start a forest fire.

The words you speak to a person may not seem to be all that spectacular to your own ears. They may be words that you are sure that person has heard many times. You may not even feel particularly empowered as you speak. And yet, the miracle of hearing may very well occur for that person. That's the result of the Holy Spirit preparing his ears to hear.

> THE WORDS YOU SPEAK TO A PERSON MAY NOT SEEM ALL THAT SPECTACULAR TO YOUR OWN EARS, YET THE MIRACLE OF HEARING MAY VERY WELL OCCUR FOR THAT PERSON.

Consider the example of lighting a match in order to light a candle. If the wick on the candle isn't ready to receive a flame, the match will just blaze and die. The failure to light the candle does not lie in the match but in the candle. And even if the match fails to light the candle, it has—for one brief moment—provided light. So it is with your words. Even if the other person doesn't receive your words, the words have been spoken as rays of light into darkness.

Who knows who may have overheard your words? Your prayer? The verse you gave? The word of testimony you shared?

And, even more important, who knows the ability of the Spirit of God to penetrate hearts in ways we can't even imagine?

Years ago, I led a man to Christ as we prayed together over the telephone. I was in the reception area of a car dealership owned by a friend of mine.

After praying with the man over the phone, I noticed a lady in the waiting area who had been listening to my conversation as I'd shared the gospel and prayed with him.

So, I asked the lady if she had ever received Christ into her life. She said, "Yes." "How long ago?" I asked. "Just a few minutes ago, as you prayed with the person on the phone," she replied. "I prayed with you and asked the Lord to save me, too, and to come into my life."

God often does more than we can even ask or think! (See Ephesians 3:20.)

Questions for Reflection and/or Discussion

1. What four things does God equip and expect us to do as we participate in His work of salvation?

2. Discuss the place of prayer in effectively introducing others to Christ, including the following: What should you pray for? What does prayer do for you? When should you pray regarding your activities in reaching out to others with the gospel?

3. In what ways does the devil attempt to hinder people from being open to the gospel? How does prayer counteract these attacks?

4. How does your worship affect your witness?

5. Discuss the importance of living a consistent, Christlike life.

6. What content should be included when you share your testimony?

7. Why is it so important to know and meditate on the Word of God?

8. What are some ways in which you can hide God's Word in your heart?

9. What are some passages of Scripture that would be good to memorize or have available in sharing the gospel?

10. Why should the cross of Christ be a focal point in presenting the gospel?

11. Name a few things you can expect the Holy Spirit to do as you share God's Word with others.

— 6 —

EMBRACING GOD'S CALL

According to a Barna Group survey, "a slight majority of born again adults—55%—claimed to have shared their faith in Christ with a non-Christian during the prior 12 months. That figure has remained relatively constant during the past decade."[1] Many people are hungering for the word of eternal life, but about half of adult believers are not offering the Bread of Life, Jesus, to satisfy that hunger.

Proving God's Faithfulness

A man recently said to me, "I pray all the time that God will use me to bring people to Christ, but I never seem to come across people with prepared hearts."

I said to him, "I think it's about time you put the Lord to the test."

He said, "What do you mean?"

"Well, if you've been praying that He will use you to lead others to Christ, how are you going to know if He's answering your prayer unless you open up a conversation with others about the Lord?"

He didn't say anything, but I could see the gears spinning in his mind, so I continued, "The Lord may have put dozens of people across your path, carefully arranging and orchestrating their lives just so they'd be in close proximity to you—people whose hearts were ready to receive Christ Jesus and be born anew spiritually. How will you ever know what the Lord is doing if you don't test the situation by speaking up and asking people if they have been thinking about the Lord lately, or some similar question?"

He said, "I never thought of it that way."

Most people don't. They are more afraid of sharks swimming in the waters of un-entered conversations than they are joyful at the prospect that drowning souls might be saved from those waters!

Stop to think about it for a minute. The Lord is far more concerned about bringing people to His Son than you are. He wants people to be saved from eternal damnation and to receive eternal life much more than you do.

If, indeed, you have been praying in faith that God would use you to share Christ with others, why wouldn't the Lord cause someone to gravitate your way to…

- be called in an emergency to do a double shift just so he'll be available when you arrive on the scene?

- be the clerk who responds to you in a store that's filled with dozens of clerks?

- be the taxi driver who comes to the airport and gets you as a passenger, rather than any of a thousand other travelers?

- take a different route home so his path will intersect with yours?

- stop to pick up a loaf of bread in the same store in which you've stopped for a carton of milk?

When you make yourself available to the Lord, He delights in sending people your way for the purpose of allowing you to share His life with them. Trust Him to arrange the circumstances and the encounters. However, you won't know if the Lord has sent a person your way unless you put the situation to the test. So, open up a conversation about Christ Jesus and testify of Him.

Spontaneous Witness

Our witness of Jesus Christ flows from our union with Him. It's a matter of being in a right relationship with Him and letting Him demonstrate who He is through our humanity.

Being a spontaneous witness should be a normal part of the life of Christ's followers. When we are totally available to the Lord, He will express His love, wisdom, and power to those around us.

It's not a matter of working up or praying down the presence of Christ; instead, it's a matter of acting on God's revealed truth and discovering His adequacy in every life experience.

Sharing Christ with Others Is Intentional

Attempting to bring others into a relationship with Christ is not accidental. (Some witnessing opportunities, however, seem accidental—at least from our human viewpoint. There are times when we find ourselves sharing about Christ almost before we have time to think about what we are saying.)

Seeking to introduce others to Christ involves:

+ a frame of mind—that you are going to share Christ at every appropriate opportunity.

+ a world perspective—that all people need to hear the good news of Jesus Christ.

+ focused concentration—that you'll continually be alert for someone to tell about the Lord Jesus.

+ purpose—that you intend all of your words and deeds to honor Christ.

Let's consider God's promise in Mark 1:17 that, if we follow Christ, He will make us *"fishers of men."* We know that catching fish doesn't happen by accident. Fish don't just leap out of a pond or lake and land on your doorstep fifteen miles away.

To catch fish, you must do the following:

1. Decide that you are going fishing. A fisherman sets his mind and heart toward that activity. He says, "I'm going fishing."

2. Get to a body of water where you believe you'll find fish. The fisherman puts himself into position to catch fish.

3. Choose a spot. It might mean choosing a depth if you are trolling the lake, but, even so, you will gravitate toward certain coves and inlets. Nearly every fisherman has a favorite "fishing hole" that is in one specific location in a lake, pond, stream, or river.

4. Prepare your gear and your bait for the type of fish you are attempting to hook. And cast in your line!

Each of these principles is directly related to bringing people into the kingdom of God—being fishers of men.

Decide That You're Going to Share Christ

Adopt a mind-set that says, "I'm going to be continually on the alert for someone with whom I might share the gospel."

So few people have adopted this mind-set. And yet, it's the number one step to introducing people to Jesus Christ.

I'm talking about something far more than saying, "Let's go door-to-door with tracts on Tuesday night next week." Granted, that's an intentional approach. It's also much more limited than what I am suggesting.

I'm suggesting that you have a "share Christ" perspective every hour of every day:

- When you take that out-of-town business trip, expect the Lord to provide opportunities to show and share the love of Christ.

- When you go into a store, expect to share Christ with someone.

- When you eat in a restaurant, be alert for opportunities to engage in spiritual conversations. (However, it's important to be sensitive to the situation. Don't interfere with someone's job or work. A busy mealtime may not be the best time to approach the servers.)

Sharing the good news in an intentional way isn't an automatic response to your life in Christ. To adopt this mind-set is to *train your mind* to think in this way. It's not a habit that comes with your spiritual conversion. It's a habit that comes through both the transformation of your life and the discipline of your mind.

Talking about your life in Christ is a choice of your will. It's intending to lead others to Him. It's setting your face and your life toward that activity. It's making a total commitment to Christ and His kingdom purposes.

Once you make this commitment...

> SHARING THE GOOD NEWS IN AN INTENTIONAL WAY IS A HABIT THAT COMES THROUGH BOTH THE TRANSFORMATION OF YOUR LIFE AND THE DISCIPLINE OF YOUR MIND.

Expect Your Steps to Be Directed

The Word of God says, *"A man's heart plans his way, but the LORD directs his steps"* (Proverbs 16:9).

When you make a commitment to sharing your faith, that's an act of "planning your way." You are setting your heart, your will, toward Christ. And when you do, the Lord will direct your specific steps, setting up individual encounters for you and putting people into your path whose hearts are prepared to accept the message you have to give.

One of the major reasons many believers do not share their faith is that they have preconceived ideas about the way others might respond if they made the effort. The negative stereotype of confrontational evangelism often becomes a hurdle in reaching out to others.

Pray for Boldness

The apostle Paul, whom many regard as the boldest of all preachers in the first century, prayed for boldness and asked others to pray that he might speak boldly about Christ.

In his letter to the Ephesians, Paul vividly described the *"whole armor of God"* (Ephesians 6:13) and our need to wear this armor as we fight against *"spiritual hosts of wickedness in the heavenly places"* (verse 12) and *"withstand in the evil day"* (verse 13). What are we to do once we have donned this armor? Pray. Be watchful. Share Christ intentionally and confidently.

Praying always with all prayer and supplication in the Spirit, being watchful to this end with all perseverance and supplication for all the saints; and for me, that utterance may be given to me, that I may open my mouth boldly to make known the mystery of the gospel, for which I am an ambassador in chains; that in it I may speak boldly, as I ought to speak. (Ephesians 6:18–20)

The apostle Peter, who preached the great sermon on the day of Pentecost that resulted in three thousand souls being added to the kingdom, was later arrested with John for healing a lame man. He and John were thrown into prison overnight, grilled by the religious leaders of the city the next day, and then released with a stern warning never to preach about Jesus again. When their fellow believers heard of all this, they prayed for Peter and John, *"Now, Lord, look on their threats, and grant to Your servants that with all boldness they may speak Your word"* (Acts 4:29). The Scriptures go on to say that after they had prayed, they were *"filled with the Holy Spirit, and they spoke the word of God with boldness"* (verse 31).

Do you lack boldness today in sharing Jesus Christ with others? Ask God to give you boldness. If the apostle Paul felt the need to pray for boldness, then, certainly, we should, also. God is ready, willing, and able to answer your prayer for boldness.

Boldness Is Born of Love

In his first letter, the apostle John wrote,

Love has been perfected among us in this: that we may have boldness in the day of judgment; because as He is, so are we in this world. There is no fear in love; but perfect love casts out fear, because fear involves torment. But he who fears has not been made perfect in love. (1 John 4:17–18)

Your lack of boldness is very likely related to a lack of love for others and a lack of awareness of God's love for you.

Most of us don't like to face that fact. We like to see ourselves as being loving, generous-hearted, willing-to-sacrifice-for-others people.

The truth is that most of us are still looking out for number one. We're more concerned about what other people will think of us than we are about how the Lord desires to love other people through us.

Ask the Lord to give you a renewed, dynamic, deep, and compassionate love for other people. Make it your desire to love people as Jesus loves them.

> ASK THE LORD TO GIVE YOU A RENEWED, DYNAMIC, DEEP, AND COMPASSIONATE LOVE FOR OTHER PEOPLE.

God Is the Source of Love

Love is the foremost characteristic that is given to us by the Holy Spirit, as Romans 5:5 declares: *"The love of God has been poured out in our hearts by the Holy Spirit who was given to us."*

The Bible defines the very nature of God as being one of love. (See 1 John 4:8, 16.) To grow in your love for others is really to allow more of the love of Jesus Christ to be manifested in your life. It is to receive love in such a way that it overflows to others.

Stop to consider what it truly means to you to be saved. Consider what your destiny would be if you did not know the Lord; ponder the fact of everlasting separation from your heavenly Father and of eternal death. Try to imagine what your life would be like if you didn't know Jesus Christ—if you had no means of forgiveness and no Holy Spirit from whom to draw wisdom, counsel, and help.

That is the existence of those who have not received the Lord into their lives.

Will you allow the love of Jesus to flow through you to them and, in doing so, to conquer all your fear of rejection or ridicule?

Did you know...

You Can Share Your Faith Effectively

Many people readily admit, "I have a hard time motivating myself to talk about Jesus to other people."

Let me emphasize again that one of the reasons most people never share their faith is their preconceived idea of how others might respond if they made the effort.

+ They are more concerned about their own reputations than about the eternal spiritual fate and current human condition of the other person.

+ They are more concerned about what they are going to say or do than about what the other person needs to hear or receive.

+ They are more concerned about being rejected than about the other person's feelings of dejection.

+ They are more concerned about who they are than about who that other person might become in Christ Jesus.

One of the keys to becoming motivated to share Christ is to see other people as Christ sees them. In other words, we must begin to see with His eyes.

Begin to See Other People as They Really Are

I challenge you to conduct your own personal survey.

Look into the faces of people as they stand waiting for a bus or subway. Look into the faces of people as they sit in an airport waiting lounge or a hotel lobby. Watch the faces of those whom you see in a restaurant, in the mall, or on the freeway.

You will see a lot of sadness and misery in those faces.

Seldom will you see someone who has a pleasant expression on his face, much less a smile. Most of the faces convey worry, sadness, despair, exhaustion, anger, frustration, fear, or just plain ol' trouble.

The Scriptures tell us again and again that Jesus was moved with compassion as He saw the needs of the multitudes and of individuals. (See, for example, Matthew 9:36; Mark 1:40–42.)

We have compassion for others when we begin to see them as they truly are.

Again, look into the eyes of people as you encounter them walking along a busy sidewalk. Look into the eyes of clerks as they wait on you. Look into the eyes of waiters and waitresses as they take your order. In most cases, you will *not* see joy in their eyes or sense real peace in their lives.

Start seeing the people around you with new eyes. Ask the Lord to enable you to see them from His perspective.

The Hurdle of Anticipated Failure

Sometimes, people think their past failures or reputations will get in the way of their witness. Once more, our preconceived ideas often keep us from taking that step of faith and reaching out to others.

Don't let a past failure, mistake, or error be held up to you by the enemy of your soul as something that prohibits you from telling another person about Jesus Christ. What the Lord has done in your heart to save you, deliver you, or heal you from that circumstance, addiction, instance, or relationship is what really matters. Focus on Christ and what *He* has done.

> DON'T LET A PAST FAILURE OR MISTAKE PREVENT YOU FROM TELLING ANOTHER PERSON ABOUT JESUS CHRIST AND HOW HE HAS SAVED YOU.

There's also a hurdle of "insufficiency" or "lack of ability" that some people put in their own paths. They don't feel that they are worthy to express the gospel. In fact, they aren't. None of us is! But Jesus is worthy to be expressed! He is the Good News.

The Scriptures say that we are *"sufficient as ministers of the new covenant* [*"new testament"* KJV]" (2 Corinthians 3:6). You *are* capable because of His indwelling life.

The Hurdle of Good Intentions

Another hurdle is that of good intentions. Let me assure you, however, that good intentions alone haven't yet led a person to the Lord!

Don't relegate your witness to something that will happen in the future...

- ✦ "When I'm strong enough in the Lord."
- ✦ "When I overcome this trial."
- ✦ "When I'm good enough to be His witness."
- ✦ "When I've grown enough in the faith."
- ✦ "When I've learned enough of the Bible."
- ✦ "When I've been a member of the church longer."

There's no prerequisite of training, time, experience, knowledge, membership, or accomplishment to share your faith.

There's only the desire to see lost, hurting, and defeated people experience what you have experienced in the Lord.

Finally, there's the biggest hurdle of all—at least it's the one that I see the most people grappling with…

The Hurdle of Fear

I once read an article in which the author reported having conducted a study that revealed 90 percent of all fears have no basis in reality. Fear grips the mind. It torments. It restricts and binds. It causes us to limit what we do and say for the Lord.

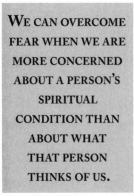

WE CAN OVERCOME FEAR WHEN WE ARE MORE CONCERNED ABOUT A PERSON'S SPIRITUAL CONDITION THAN ABOUT WHAT THAT PERSON THINKS OF US.

The fear of failure or rejection keeps many from sharing their faith.

We can overcome fear when we are more concerned about a person's spiritual condition and eternal destiny than we are about what that person thinks of us.

Remember that perfect love casts out fear.

The love and grace of God will enable you to reach out and share His life with confidence.

Second Timothy 1:7 says, *"For God has not given us a spirit of fear, but of power and of love and of a sound mind."* Say, as Queen Esther said, *"If I perish, I perish!"* (Esther 4:16). The alternative was for all of Esther's people to be annihilated.

Confront the reality head-on.

The Good News about Hurdles

The good news about these hurdles is that the Holy Spirit can and will enable us to overcome them if we will trust God and obey His Word.

We so often preoccupy ourselves with various activities and secondary causes without seeing those things as opportunities to demonstrate the love of Christ.

For some of us, our concern for sharing Christ will involve resetting our priorities to line up with God's kingdom priorities.

Finally...

Recognize That Bringing Others to Christ Is a Great Privilege

I believe God puts it in our hearts and gives us the grace and the enabling to make a significant contribution to the advancement of the kingdom of God. I believe every true believer has an inner desire and motivation to make a difference for the cause of Christ. Unfortunately, it is never realized and released in many of us because of unbelief or disobedience, or a lack of understanding of the ways of God.

When we are rightly related to the Lord Jesus and identified with His plans and purposes, we will have a passion to be used by Him.

You Have What It Takes

You don't need to be a scholar in order to lead others to Christ.

You don't need to be a preacher.

You don't need to be ordained as a pastor.

You don't need to have a degree in theology or even to have completed a Bible training course.

You don't need to have been a church member for many years.

You don't need to be a great public speaker.

It doesn't take a great deal of skill to express your faith to others. It takes a desire to share Jesus with those who need Him. Again, let me emphasize the fact that there is great value in training and skill development. However, every person who has a relationship with the Lord can begin to share his life in Christ where he is right now, regardless of his training or education.

Some of the most effective men and women of God throughout history have been those who did not have very much formal education. But what they did have was a heart for the Lord and a passion to see others come to Christ. (See 1 Corinthians 1:26–31.)

There's no greater joy.

Questions for Reflection and/or Discussion

1. Where are some good places to find people to reach out to with the love of Christ?

2. Discuss what it means to be a "fisher of men."

3. Who should take the initiative when it comes to sharing Christ?

4. How does your mind-set or attitude toward others affect your ability to recognize witness or ministry opportunities?

5. Discuss what it means to be an intentional witness.

6. What are some of the hurdles or barriers to effectively sharing Christ?

7. What is the source of boldness in witnessing?

8. Why do many Christians never lead anyone to Christ?

9. How can we overcome the fear of witnessing?

10. How can you better line up your life with kingdom priorities?

11. What were the qualities of some of the most effective men and women of God throughout history?

—7—

GETTING STARTED

Perhaps much of what we have discussed so far has been familiar to you. I hope that's true!

As we move into the area of methods and technique, I'd like to share a word of caution. It's very easy to fall into a pattern of doing things by relying on human ability and memory. It's important to recognize that our efforts at sharing Christ must depend upon the work of the Holy Spirit. Methods and techniques can become substitutes for spiritual sensitivity. I hope you will be aware of that fact as you read the remaining chapters of this book.

Keep these thoughts in mind:

+ Don't think you have to persuade or convince someone to make a decision or pray a prayer.

+ Don't be more concerned about presenting the plan of salvation than the Man of salvation—Jesus.

+ Don't worry about presenting people with steps or formulas but rather introduce them to the person of Jesus Christ.

A relationship with the Lord Jesus is a spiritual matter. Witnessing techniques should always flow from that relationship and not be isolated as a pattern to follow, with "one size fits all" as its motto.

Where Do You Find Ministry Opportunities?

Years ago, I got to know a pastor who had come across my first book about helping others to know Christ. The book had inspired him to be more intentional about sharing Christ outside his "church field." His concept of outreach had pretty much been limited to the context of his church membership and his local geographic area.

When I met this pastor, he had just returned from an out-of-town trip and had led two people to Christ while he was away. He was very excited, and he thanked me for enlarging his horizons of ministry.

Consider all the opportunities most of us have to reach out with the love of Christ. When you meet people in various places, think of those encounters as divine appointments.

I've found that I frequently cross paths with several categories of people as I travel. The following are some examples of those whom I often encounter who need Jesus:

- Waitstaff
- Cab drivers
- Bellhops
- Hotel staff
- Security guards

When you travel a great deal, you are around these people continually. Every major city has thousands of people working in the professions named above. Surely, God can intersect your travel path with several who are ready to meet Him.

In your occupation, you'll no doubt be in regular contact with still other categories of people, such as...

- Airline passengers
- Ticket agents
- Shoppers
- Clerks

Indeed, your profession, especially if it's a service profession, will put you in touch with...

- Clients
- Vendors

- ◆ Customers

- ◆ Colleagues

If you work for a large organization, you're likely to encounter dozens of coworkers in any given day.

The opportunities are virtually endless!

Connecting with people in those short-term encounters will often result in opportunities to develop new friendships and to have an ongoing ministry. Many of those whom I've met and connected with over the years as I've traveled have become good friends, and we have stayed in touch.

Of course, for most of us, the greatest opportunities we'll have to impact the spiritual lives of others will be with those whom we are closest to. Our primary mission field will be our families, neighbors, coworkers, and friends. This is where our lifestyles and relational witness are so important.

> FOR MOST OF US, THE GREATEST OPPORTUNITIES WE'LL HAVE TO IMPACT THE SPIRITUAL LIVES OF OTHERS WILL BE WITH THOSE WHOM WE ARE CLOSEST TO.

However, in addition to those circles of influence, there are multitudes of short-term encounters in which we can speak a word of testimony or encouragement. And many times, the Lord will open a fruitful witness or ministry opportunity.

Some people working in certain companies or governmental agencies will have restrictions regarding how they can witness and talk to others about the Lord. In many situations, the most effective witness is how you treat people, how you serve them and demonstrate the love of Christ.

Settle for the fact that you can be salt and light by the way you live, and God will often open a door of ministry in His unique and creative way.

Be a Sensitive Observer

Watch people. See how they act and react. Watch their movements and the expressions on their faces.

Notice what kinds of books, magazines, or newspapers they are reading.

As you make these observations, ask the Lord to give you insight on how to best relate to a particular person.

You can tell a great deal about people just by these types of observation. Most negative emotions—sadness, sorrow, dismay, pain, fear, distrust, defeat, worry, pent-up anger, and grief—are readily portrayed in a person's physical demeanor.

Become a student of human behavior. Learn to recognize downcast eyes, hunched shoulders, furrowed brows, clenched hands (or handbags or rolled-up magazines), involuntary grimaces, and other facial and physical expressions for what they are—likely indicators of how a person is feeling on the inside.

Trust the Lord for discernment into people's spiritual needs. As you observe people and listen to the Holy Spirit, He will often give you a word of wisdom or knowledge as you begin to engage them in conversation.

God Delights in Answering Prayers to Meet People's Needs

Most of us don't hide our emotions very well. Frustration, worry, and sorrow are three strong emotions that are difficult to hide.

> MOST PEOPLE ARE NOT OFFENDED BY YOUR OFFER TO PRAY FOR THEM OR WITH THEM.

When you see people who are struggling with deep emotions, you may want to offer to pray for them or just be available to listen.

Most people are not offended by your offer to pray for them or with them. God delights in answering our prayers to meet the felt needs of people in order to reveal Himself to them.

Those encounters often provide opportunities to share the gospel. The greatest antidotes in the world for trouble are joy and peace. Jesus promised both.

Peace I leave with you, My peace I give to you; not as the world gives do I give to you. Let not your heart be troubled, neither let it be afraid.
(John 14:27)

*These things I have spoken to you, that My joy may remain in you, and
that your joy may be full.* (John 15:11)

Your sorrow will be turned into joy. (John 16:20)

Be Confident in the Lord

Perhaps the most important thing you can do as you move through this
world is to let the radiance and confidence of the Lord be seen in you. In my
opinion, followers of Christ should be the most confident people in the world.

Our confidence isn't in our own abilities. Our confidence is in the Lord.
Our confidence rests in Him and what He prompts us to do and say. The
better we get to know God, what He is like and how He works, the more
confidence we will have in His wisdom and power to work through us.

Our confidence is in knowing that Jesus Christ is our Savior and the
Lord of our lives, our sins are forgiven, we were created to bring glory to the
Lord, we were created to have dominion over the earth, and we are bound
for heaven.

Confidence born of that knowledge is true confidence! And most people are looking for someone who knows what he believes and who can state
what he believes with confidence.

Confidence Attracts

If you portray a lack of confidence in what you are saying about Jesus,
the person you are talking to is likely to tune you out—because of your
attitude rather than because of the words you are using. Confidence, however, attracts. It compels people who are seeking the Lord to want to hear
more of what you have to say about Him.

A man told me in tears one day, "I've never had anybody talk to me like
that. Thank you." And another man said, "I've never talked with anyone
who has spoken to me with such peace and authority combined. It makes
you really believable to me."

I took both of those statements as compliments about the Lord working through me. I certainly recognize it as His work, not as a skill or unique

ability I've acquired. Jesus spoke that way when He walked this earth. He was gentle and peaceful in the way He dealt with those who were sick, hurting, doubting, suffering, or bruised by society or the religious leaders of the day. He came in a spirit of binding up the brokenhearted and speaking good news to those with impoverished spirits. (See Luke 4:17–22.) That's peace! Yet, He had authority over all principalities and powers. He walked and healed and spoke with great power. (See, for example, Mark 1:22–27.) The combination is irresistible.

> GOD IS WILLING AND ABLE TO DO THROUGH US WHAT HE DID THROUGH JESUS.

Again, it's His work in us and through us. Jesus even said about Himself in His humanity, *"Most assuredly, I say to you, the Son can do nothing of Himself, but what He sees the Father do; for whatever He does, the Son also does in like manner"* (John 5:19). The same is true for us. We are to speak and do what our Father is prompting us to speak and do through the power of His Holy Spirit at work in our lives. Remember that the same God who lived in Jesus then, lives in us now. Although we can do nothing by ourselves, He is willing and able to do through us now what He did through Jesus then.

Acts 2:22 says, *"Men of Israel, hear these words: Jesus of Nazareth, a Man attested by God to you by miracles, wonders, and signs which God did through Him…."*

It is amazing to consider that what God did through Jesus, He is prepared to do through you and me as we make ourselves available to Him and act in faith and obedience.

Speak Friendly Words

It has been my experience that when I greet people in a friendly manner, they respond accordingly. I know that in today's society, there is a need to be discerning and discreet, but I believe the Holy Spirit will prompt us regarding when to speak and when not to speak.

In most situations, a smile, a word of greeting, or some comment about the weather is all it takes to connect with people.

Sometimes, that alone opens up a conversation. The other person may well ask, "Are you from around here? Are you visiting?" At other times, I initiate the conversation.

I always try to get the person's name. In areas of public service (such as waitstaff or taxi drivers), the name of the person is often displayed on a name badge or license. In beginning a conversation with a person, I use his name and then ask a question in a friendly manner.

I often ask as I meet people in various cities, "Are you from around here?" If they say they are, I ask them to tell me something about their city and, especially, to tell me if there's anything encouraging happening in the area.

Another approach I have found to be effective is asking, "Have you noticed any signs of spiritual awakening in your part of the country?" People often respond with, "What do you mean?"

So, I go on to say, "Have you noticed how many are coming to a new awareness of their need for the Lord?"

That's a more general and nonthreatening approach, but their response often gives me an indication of their own personal interest in spiritual matters.

As you engage people in conversation, listen, not only to their words, but also to their tone of voice, and notice their body language.

"Making an approach" is really nothing more than initiating a friendly conversation in what is, for the most part, an unfriendly world.

It's taking time to notice another person.

It's making contact.

It's speaking friendly words in a friendly tone.

When you stop to think about it, that's a good witness for the Lord, in and of itself! The challenge now is to turn that friendly conversation into an opportunity for a life-changing encounter.

Questions for Reflection and/or Discussion

1. Who makes up your personal mission field?

2. How does the Holy Spirit direct you to share your faith?

3. What are some indicators that someone is open to the gospel?

4. When Jesus was on earth, He spoke and did what the Father prompted Him to do. How is that same relationship meant to be repeated in us as believers today?

5. What are some ways to open a conversation around spiritual matters?

—8—

MOVING TO THE HEART
OF THE MATTER

Sharing the gospel through stories and questions enables us to reach out with the love of Christ to people who may not have any immediate contact with believers in their circle of friends and who may have no other spiritual influence in their lives, such as Christian literature or television.

A few years ago, I was sharing a meal with three friends in a restaurant. On one of the trips our waitress made to our table, I said to her, "We've got some very encouraging news to share with you, if you can come back by our table a little later when you aren't busy."

She told us her shift was about over and that she'd stop by later. Sure enough, as we ended our meal, she came by and said, "Well, here I am."

I said, "Something very exciting has happened to all four of us."

She asked, "All at the same time?"

I said, "No, all at different times, but the same thing happened to each of us."

She said, "What is it?"

I said, "We've all come to discover new life in Christ—that He died for our sins, arose from the dead, and desires to come into each of our hearts and make us a new person and give us peace, joy, and eternal life. Has that ever happened to you?"

She said, "No."

"Do you realize you need the Lord?" I asked.

She said, "Yes." And, after further explaining the gospel, we had the privilege of leading her in a prayer right there.

No sooner had we ended our prayer and started rejoicing together at her newfound life in Jesus Christ than her relief waitress came to our table. I said to her, "Bobbie, you might be interested in knowing that Suzanne just received the Lord Jesus into her heart. She's been made a new creation, and you can probably tell by her smile and the look in her eyes that she has a newfound joy inside that comes from being forgiven of her sins. You need the same thing, don't you?"

She said, "Yes, I do." And we had the opportunity to share the gospel and lead her in a prayer, too.

So Quickly? So Easily?

I don't always bring up the name of Jesus this quickly or easily, but when the Lord has prepared a person's heart, and he is receptive to the Lord, it's often just a matter of prompting him with questions. These three principles have begun to ring true for me:

+ The extension of an opportunity for a person to receive the Lord into his life need not be long or drawn out. Many times, our conversations get sidetracked to secondary issues rather than getting to the point—which is Christ and the cross.

+ More people are prepared in their hearts to receive and confess the Lord Jesus than most of us may realize. In fact, as I mentioned in the introduction to this book, there are probably more lost people who are prepared to respond to the gospel than there are believers who are intentionally reaching out to them.

+ People can receive the Lord anywhere and at any time. Alone or in a crowd. In motion or standing still. In any posture. Using a wide variety of words and phrases. The Lord sees the intent of the heart.

Examples of Conversation Starters

Through the years, I've settled on several questions that seem to work best for me in bringing a person to respond to the grace of God. Again, I share them with you with a word of caution: The important aspect of any conversation is to follow the leading of the Holy Spirit as He uses you, a unique individual, to share the good news of His Son with another unique individual. Every encounter has distinctive qualities to it.

"Is Anything Encouraging Happening?"

Two of my favorite questions to ask are these: "Is anything encouraging happening in your life?" and "Do you see anything encouraging happening around you or in the lives of people you know?"

I ask these questions as if I'm conducting my own personal survey.

Depending on the person's response, you have some clue as to how to proceed. He will often say something like, "What about you?" From there, I often share some way the Lord has worked in my own life or how God is at work in the world.

By starting with a more general statement, I find that most of the people with whom I speak remain very open.

An opening remark such as this lets the person know immediately that you are a positive person and that the conversation is going to be uplifting.

Another favorite question of mine, which I've used in some earlier examples, is this:

"Have You Noticed Any Signs of Spiritual Awakening in Your Area?"

Many times, a person will respond, "What do you mean?"

"Well, have you noticed how people are becoming more aware of their need for the Lord?"

I've had people respond by saying, "I don't know about anyone else, but I know I need the Lord."

Again, those whom you engage in conversation will often know the Lord, and it will be an opportunity for you to encourage them in their spiritual journeys.

Others will have questions, and some will be open to further discussion.

If there's any sign of responsiveness, I go ahead to share the gospel more fully with them.

Another favorite question of mine for turning a conversation to the Lord is this:

"Have You Been Thinking More about the Lord Lately?"

The more I've shared Christ with people through the years, the more I've come to realize that it doesn't take a long conversation to get to the root of a person's spiritual life.

The majority of people I've talked with have one of these reactions to such a direct question:

- ✦ If they are open and receptive to the gospel, they are grateful that the conversation has taken that turn.

- ✦ If they have questions or concerns about spiritual matters, such a question gives them an opportunity to voice them.

- ✦ If they respond negatively, we have an opportunity to show them love and respect and to keep the door open for any possible witness in the future.

BE OPEN TO THE CREATIVE LEADERSHIP OF THE HOLY SPIRIT AND REALIZE THAT THERE IS NO ONE SINGLE WAY OR FORMULA FOR INTRODUCING CHRIST INTO YOUR CONVERSATION.

If I am in a situation where I know I'll have more time, like a two- or three-hour airplane flight, I'll take more time to cultivate a relationship before moving to spiritual matters.

Or, if you will be seeing a person on other occasions, it's often more effective to get to know the person and tell him a little more about yourself.

Just be open to the creative leadership of the Holy Spirit and realize that there is no one single way or formula for introducing Christ into your conversation.

The question "Have you been thinking more about the Lord lately?" actually provides an excellent means of determining very quickly where a person is in his relationship with the Lord.

Frequently, a person will respond with something like this:

+ "Come to think of it, I have been watching a lot of Christian television lately."

+ "Yeah, my wife has been encouraging me a lot lately to go to church with her."

+ "It's interesting that you would ask that question because…." Then, he may share some personal experience.

Sometimes, the person will proceed to tell me about specific problems or circumstances in his life that have been prompting a greater concern for spiritual matters.

In nearly all of those cases, I'm able to provide a word of spiritual encouragement or to speak to the person further about the saving power of Jesus.

I recently said to a waitress, "You've been thinking about the Lord in just the last couple of days, haven't you?"

She said, "It's very strange that you should ask me that. Last night, I looked in the mirror and thought, *Lord, what's going on in my life?*"

I said, "The reason you had that thought last night is that the Lord knew you've been thinking more about Him lately, and He knew I was going to be here today, and I was going to ask you that question. Today is the day of salvation for you, and it's time for you to respond to the grace of God. Right now, you can bow your head and say, 'Lord Jesus Christ, I know I need You. Have mercy upon me, a sinner, and save me.' You are ready right now, so go ahead."

She bowed her head there at the side of the table, said those words, and received Christ into her life. Radiance flooded her face. She had come to the table to pour me a second cup of coffee; she left a new creation in Christ.

I believe that if you will sincerely pray at the start of the day,

Heavenly Father, use me today. Lead me to people with whom I can share the good news of Your Son. Give me an opportunity to lift up Your name,

then God will answer your prayer! He will bring you into contact with those who are ready to hear about Jesus Christ.

The Lord seems to delight in putting the right people in just the right place at the right time for His divine purposes.

"Has the Lord Been Good to You Today?"

A simple approach and greeting I have used over the years that has been instrumental in opening up conversations about the Lord is, "Has the Lord been good to you today?" I'm amazed at all the different responses I have gotten.

I will never forget a lady to whom I asked that question one time. Her immediate and stern response was, "No!"

"Do you wonder why?" I asked her. Christina thought she didn't deserve anything good from God and was obviously living under a lot of guilt.

I asked her if she was aware that Jesus Christ had died on the cross for her and had been raised from the dead so she could be free from her own guilt, be forgiven of her sins, and have a new start in life. She said that she had never received Christ but did know something about the gospel message. After further explaining the gospel to her, I led her in prayer, and she confessed Christ and called upon Him to forgive her and save her. I could sense a real change in her spirit as we prayed.

MANY PEOPLE ARE LIVING UNDER THE GUILT OF SIN AND HURT, WAITING FOR SOMEONE TO SHARE WITH THEM THE WAY OUT THROUGH CHRIST.

After we prayed together, she said, "Why didn't you come sooner? I wish I had done this long ago!" Christina was filled with joy and thanksgiving as we left the restaurant. In that brief encounter, the Lord had made a dramatic change in both her life and attitude.

There are so many like Christina, living under the guilt of sin and hurt, just waiting for someone to share with them the way out through the Lord Jesus Christ.

I have a friend who uses this approach to open a conversation with a person:

"Has Anyone Told You Today That God Loves You?"

If the person says yes (which is unlikely), my friend follows up with, "Well, let me add my witness to theirs. God truly does love you." He might then ask the person if he knows the Lord or seek to encourage him if he already knows the Lord.

If the person says no, he has an open door to say, "Well, God *does* love you. In fact, He loves you so much that He sent His Son, Jesus, to die on the cross for your sins so that you can be forgiven and freed from guilt, have peace and joy in your life, and live with the Lord forever in heaven."

This man leads many people to the Lord, nearly all of whom are introduced to the gospel in conversations that are opened with that very simple, nonconfrontational, lovingly asked question.

Ever since I met this man and heard about his approach, I've used it on many occasions and found that it works for me, too.

One Formula Doesn't Fit All

God is a creative God. He seldom does exactly the same thing twice.

The same is true in the way He leads each of us to a greater understanding of Himself.

As you converse with people, be aware of their uniqueness. Catch a glimpse of how God has been working in their lives, and catch a glimpse of who they are. Ask the Holy Spirit to reveal to you a little of His plan and purpose for their lives.

Acknowledge that their gifts and talents come from the Lord. Note the way they express themselves—in their dress, their words, their mannerisms. Their creativity is a gift from God.

Notice whether they speak with an accent. Where are they from? What is their background? What has led them to the place where you encountered them?

Recognize that our heavenly Father has put them in specific jobs, careers, or work situations, and has surrounded them with unique relationships, all in His effort to create in them an awareness of their need and to bring them to a saving knowledge of His Son, Jesus Christ.

Recognize that God is working all things in agreement with the decision of His own will. (See Ephesians 1:11.)

> EACH INCIDENT, EACH ENCOUNTER, EACH CONVERSATION, EACH PERSON IS DISTINCTIVE.

There really are no chance encounters with God. We can have confidence that when we are surrendered to the lordship of Jesus Christ and filled with the Holy Spirit, He will connect us with people in order to advance His redemptive purposes.

Each incident, each encounter, each conversation, each person is distinctive.

Discover What Fits You Best

Over the years, people have asked me, "What do I say?" or "How do I get started in sharing Christ?"

Be open to learn all you can from others whom the Lord has used, both in contemporary society and throughout history.

Don't be afraid to try what works for another person. You'll discover quickly whether you are comfortable with an approach and whether it leads to conversations about the Lord that result in others coming to know Him. You may try several approaches before you discover the one that works best for you. You may also find the Lord leading you to use one approach for a period of time, or in certain situations, and yet another approach during another season or in other circumstances in your life.

Avoid getting locked into any one method. Remember always that the Lord Jesus used many methods in His ministry. He approached each person as a distinctive individual, even though the overall tenor and message of His ministry had great consistency.

Finally, one of my favorite approaches is to take on the role of…

A Good-News Reporter

There's so much bad news coming at us from all sides that nearly every person appreciates a word of good news.

I once greeted a man in the hallway of an office building, and, since we were in a lingering moment, I asked him, "Do you know of any good news?" He said, "No, how about you?"

That brief encounter opened the door for me to share the good news of Jesus with that man. We prayed together, and he received Christ.

It turned out that the man knew about Jesus and had attended church for years but had never personally embraced the gospel for himself. He was filled with joy to discover the difference between being religious and having a relationship with Christ.

The seed of God's Word was planted in his heart. His Word will not return void. It will accomplish what pleases the Lord and will prosper in His purpose. (See Isaiah 55:11.)

As you share the gospel, you will marvel at God's unfolding purposes and at what He accomplishes through the lives of those to whom you witness.

I shared the gospel with Ashook, a college student from a south Asian country, and prayed with him to receive Christ. He then shared the good news with a friend of his, whom we will call Abdul, who was a graduate student from another country in south Asia.

Abdul contacted me, and after two lengthy conversations, he trusted Christ, became involved in a Bible study I was leading, and later joined the staff of the ministry I worked with at the time.

Abdul went on to translate a through-the-Bible devotional commentary into his mother language, and it was distributed throughout his home country. It was the first ever publication of its kind in that language. He later went on to seminary and became a missionary.

Be a Sower of the Gospel

So, become a sower of the gospel. In the physical realm, planting seeds in a garden is an act of faith. Many seeds may grow into plants, and others

> **IT'S WORTH SOWING THE SEED OF THE WORD BECAUSE YOU NEVER KNOW WHO HAS GOOD GROUND IN HIS HEART AND IS JUST WAITING FOR IT.**

may not, but you still plant them. The parable of the sower in Matthew 13 describes different types of ground that receive the seed of the Word of God. Some are ready for it; some are not. Some receive it only temporarily; in others, it takes lasting root. The point is that it's worth sowing the seed of the Word because you never know who has good ground in his heart and is just waiting for it.

Take on this attitude as you face tomorrow. Go from your home determined to tell others about Jesus, as if you are planting seeds. Trust God to bring forth trees that will be planted by the rivers of water. (See Psalm 1.)

Questions for Reflection and/or Discussion

1. How can you determine someone's level of interest in the Lord?

2. Why is it important to ask questions and listen before seeking to share faith in Christ with others?

3. Give some examples of questions that help in sharing one's faith.

4. What specific questions do you find most effective in sharing your faith?

5. How can you better see people's distinctiveness and note God's creative activity in their lives?

—9—

DISCERNING MINISTRY OPPORTUNITIES

Have you ever watched an expert shopper in the produce section of a grocery store?

She carefully sorts the fruits and vegetables displayed there, picking up this one and that one, discerning which ones are ripe and at their prime.

The farmer goes through the same process at harvest—checking daily, sometimes even hourly, for the sugar content of a crop to reach the optimum level, for the maximum percentage of produce to be ripe, for the heads of grain to burst open.

Perhaps unfortunately, ripe souls—those who are ready to receive Jesus—are not as easily discernible as market produce or agricultural crops.

The Readiness Test for a Soul

The only way you know who is ready to receive the Lord into his life is to ask a question, such as "Would you like to receive the Lord Jesus into your life?" or "Are you aware of your need for the Lord?"

On the surface, you can't tell who is ready and who isn't. The Holy Spirit operates at a deep level in a person's life. The readiness of a person to receive Jesus Christ cannot be seen in his dress, possessions, line of work, sex, age, or race. It is frequently not discernible by facial expressions, stress level, relationships, or even behavior. Some of the most successful-looking or successful-acting people are miserable inside and are seeking a peace of heart that only the Lord can provide. Some of those who say and do all the

115

right things in society are aching for an opportunity to find greater meaning in their lives. And, some of those who seem the most rebellious against God, in word or deed, are at a place in their souls where they are not only ready, but also eager, to repent and enter into a newness of life.

Therefore...

+ Don't prejudge a person by his outer appearance.

+ Don't prejudge a person by his behavior.

+ Don't prejudge a person by his words.

> **THE HOLY SPIRIT WILL REVEAL THE READINESS OF A PERSON'S HEART AS YOU ENTER INTO A CONVERSATION WITH HIM ABOUT JESUS CHRIST.**

The readiness level of a heart to respond to the Lord is known only to the Holy Spirit. And the Holy Spirit will reveal the heart's readiness to you only as you enter into a life-changing conversation with the person about Jesus Christ.

Let me elaborate on this point a little further. The secrets of a person's heart are known only to that person and to God's Spirit. The Scriptures say that it is the Lord who *"searches all hearts and understands all the intent of the thoughts"* (1 Chronicles 28:9).

The apostle Paul wrote to the church at Corinth,

"Eye has not seen, nor ear heard, nor have entered into the heart of man the things which God has prepared for those who love Him." But God has revealed them to us through His Spirit. For the Spirit searches all things, yes, the deep things of God. For what man knows the things of a man except the spirit of the man which is in him? Even so no one knows the things of God except the Spirit of God. Now we have received, not the spirit of the world, but the Spirit who is from God, that we might know the things that have been freely given to us by God.
(1 Corinthians 2:9–12)

The inner spirit of another person can only be discerned spiritually. And, spiritual discernment is one of the gifts of the Holy Spirit. (See also 1 Corinthians 12:10.)

Your Greatest Tool and Ally in Sharing Christ

The Word of God is your greatest tool. As you share the Word, your greatest ally is the Holy Spirit. His is the work of winning the lost—of preparing hearts, of transforming lives. You are invited to work alongside Him in a process in which He is already actively engaged!

The Holy Spirit desires that a person receive Christ Jesus far more than you do, and He will move within you and within the other person— as much as He is allowed to work—to bring the person into the family of God.

It is the Holy Spirit who "gifts" you with power and other spiritual qualities you may need to engage in sharing Christ.

Acts 1:8 tells us,

But you shall receive power when the Holy Spirit has come upon you; and you shall be witnesses to Me in Jerusalem, and in all Judea and Samaria, and to the end of the earth.

If you have received Jesus into your life and are indwelt by His Holy Spirit, then you are His witness. It's one of the main purposes for which His Holy Spirit dwells in you.

I mentioned previously that, through the years, some people have said to me, "Well, Jerry, you're just gifted to share Christ with others."

"Yes," I respond, "I have been gifted by the Holy Spirit to be His witness, just as every other follower of Christ has been gifted by the Holy Spirit to be His witness."

> EVERY BELIEVER IS EQUIPPED BY THE HOLY SPIRIT'S INDWELLING PRESENCE TO BE A FRUITFUL WITNESS.

While some believers may seem to be more gifted than others at leading people to Christ, every believer is equipped by the Holy Spirit's indwelling presence to be a fruitful witness and to share the gospel with others.

Spiritual Discernment Is Vitally Important

"Well," you may say, "I accept that I'm gifted by the Holy Spirit, but I don't seem to be gifted with spiritual discernment."

When people say that to me, I generally respond, "How do you know?"

I have described the fact that, from my experience, the gift of discerning another person's spiritual condition is most evident once you have opened a conversation with someone about the Lord Jesus. Prior to such a conversation, I seldom have many clues from the Holy Spirit about what He is doing in a person's life. It simply isn't possible—or advisable—to try to "read" a person's spiritual state apart from your conversation with him about the Lord. You may be able to discern to some degree a person's "openness" as you approach him, but you can never fully discern his spiritual relationship with our heavenly Father.

In order to activate the gift of "discerning of spirits" in your life, you must first be willing to speak the name of Jesus, for it is at and to the name of Jesus that the spirit of a person responds.

If that person is not ready to receive the Lord, he will quickly respond toward that end when the name of Jesus is spoken. He may mutter some excuse to get away from you. Or, he may attempt to change the topic of conversation very quickly—frequently to something as neutral as the weather, and sometimes to a topic that is more of a social issue than a matter of salvation. A few people react vehemently to the mention of His name.

At the opposite end of the spectrum are those who will respond to the name of Jesus with tears, or with a facial expression and other body language that give you an impression they are clinging to your every word, or that they are searching for something of great value.   I suggest to you that such an overt, positive response to the name of Jesus will cause you to discern quite clearly that the spirit of this person is open to the Lord Jesus.

In all cases, the response of a person to the name of Jesus will be such that you will be able to discern clearly his spiritual condition.

In between these extremes are those who respond in what appears to be a neutral or slightly favorable way. They may raise questions about Jesus, begin to talk about their church affiliation, or tell you about a spiritual event in their past.

In general, you can "discern" from their response that they are not closed to the Lord, and you can proceed with a conversation about Him. How you proceed is a question to ask the Holy Spirit!

"Holy Spirit, What Shall I Say?"

Perhaps the most effective prayer you can ever pray as you converse with someone about the Lord Jesus is this:

Holy Spirit, help me. Show me what You are doing in this person's life. Let me be sensitive to his need for You. Give me Your words to say!

Trust the Holy Spirit's enabling throughout your conversation with a person. Continually anticipate in your spirit, *What does Jesus Himself want to do in this situation to reconcile this person to our heavenly Father?* or *How does Jesus want to speak through me now?*

> TRUST THE HOLY SPIRIT'S ENABLING THROUGHOUT YOUR CONVERSATION WITH A PERSON.

Watch for the Holy Spirit to Give You a "Spiritual Prompting"

The Scriptures say, *"That the righteous requirement of the law might be fulfilled in us who do not walk according to the flesh but according to the Spirit"* (Romans 8:4). The *"righteous requirement of the law"* is the expression of the life of Jesus Christ in our lives. Jesus is the fulfillment of the law. He is our righteousness. He lives in us. He is our life. The righteousness of the Lord Jesus is expressed through us as we choose to walk according to the Spirit.

What does this mean to us in regard to sharing Christ?

It means that the Holy Spirit has designed a way in which He desires for us to walk after Him as we share Christ. The words I most often use in describing this are "spiritual prompting."

Have you ever watched a group of children presenting a school play? Nearly always, there's a teacher offstage or in the orchestra pit who is available to feed the little actors lines—lines so easily forgotten under the bright stage lights and with the excitement of standing before an audience.

We're in that same position, only more so. We, as little children following after the Spirit, don't have pre-rehearsed lines. *All* of our lines need to come from the Divine Prompter!

We feel virtually compelled to say the lines He gives to us.

The lines He gives to us are frequently portions of Scripture that have been hidden away in our hearts.

The lines He gives to us are the ones that woo that person and extend God's genuine love to him; they do not condemn. Very often, this compassion far exceeds what we might normally feel.

The lines He gives to us are sometimes surprising to us.

Once, I was talking with a man about spiritual matters when I suddenly felt compelled to ask him a question that, within the context of our conversation thus far, seemed totally unrelated. I said, "The real root of the problem is [and I named the problem], isn't it?" He looked at me with a little surprise and then said, genuinely, "Yes. That's really the problem." Recognizing the root of the problem allowed us to move very quickly in dealing with it. Within a few minutes, he was ready to receive the Lord into his life.

The Holy Spirit is willing and able to reveal to us areas of spiritual bondage in people's lives so that we can deal with those root issues.

As the Holy Spirit leads us, we obey. We choose to follow and act on His promptings. We become sensitive to His direction, and we open our mouths and speak—boldly, with authority, and yet warmly and gently. Even as we speak, we are silently asking the Lord to give us His next words. We listen closely to how the person responds, and we listen closely to the Spirit to see what further truth He would have us to share.

The Holy Spirit's Guidance System

How does this prompting by the Holy Spirit manifest itself? Let me give you a very practical explanation.

Do you ever find yourself watching someone? Do you feel drawn to him in some way? Assume that it is the Holy Spirit who is leading you toward that person.

Do you ever have a feeling that you understand a person whom you are watching from afar just by reading his facial expressions? Assume that it is the Holy Spirit who is giving you that understanding.

Do you sense something beneath the surface level of a person's words—perhaps a feeling of pain, worry, or uneasiness? Assume that the Holy Spirit is the One who is giving you empathy with that person.

If your assumptions are incorrect, and it isn't the Holy Spirit at work, you'll quickly discover that as you act on your assumptions!

In most cases, I like to spend a few minutes getting to know a person and asking some questions so I get a feel for what he may or may not know about the Lord. Generally speaking, I'm looking for the "gaps" in his life. I'm looking for what he doesn't know about the Lord. Then, I seek to fill in those gaps.

As I engage in conversation with a person, I'm continually looking for what more the Holy Spirit might add to this person's life. If he already knows the Lord, I'm looking for a way the Holy Spirit might bless or encourage him in his spiritual growth. If he doesn't know the Lord, I'm looking for an entry point to share more of the gospel.

> **AS YOU ENGAGE IN CONVERSATION WITH PEOPLE, CONTINUALLY LOOK FOR WHAT MORE THE HOLY SPIRIT MIGHT ADD TO THEIR LIVES.**

Did you ever study chemistry? Much of a chemistry class involves identifying unknowns. The teacher gives a sample of a compound to a class and tells the students what kinds of tests to perform in order to evaluate the compound's properties and deduce its chemical makeup.

Engaging in a conversation about Christ is very much like chemistry class—you identify the spiritual unknowns about a person. Determine his relationship with the Lord, and then, under the guidance of the Holy Spirit, help move that person ever closer to faith in Christ.

Asking the Holy Spirit to Lead You Begins Long before Your Encounter

The passage in Romans that tells us we are the fulfillment of the *"righteous requirement of the law"* (Romans 8:4) goes on to say, *"For as many as are led by the Spirit of God, these are sons of God"* (verse 14).

How can you know with assurance that you are being led and have been led?

It's possible only if you are willing to act on what you perceive to be His promptings in your heart.

Let me put this in simple terms. You pray as you get up in the morning, "Lord, will You enable me to share my life in Christ with others? Lead me today. Guide my steps. Direct me to where You want me to go, and show me what You want me to do and say. As You lead me and show me, I'll do what You direct me to do."

All through the day, you are praying this prayer. And, all through the day, you are continually on the alert for possibilities.

About four o'clock, your boss asks you to run an errand for him that's on the way to your house. He says, "Why don't you leave now to avoid the rush? No need to come back this afternoon. Go on home and bring me the item first thing in the morning." After you get the item for your boss, you stop at a convenience store to get a carton of milk. You walk into the store and get the milk from the cooler. As you prepare to pay for it, you become aware that you are alone in the store with the cashier. You suddenly realize this has never happened before, even though you've been in this store more times than you can count.

Look at the cashier's face. Watch how he is moving. What do you see? You notice that he seems very tired, hunched over, has a weary expression on his face. You sense that this man has not had a good day. You pray, "Holy Spirit, guide my words."

As you greet the cashier, you call him by the name on the tag he's wearing on his shirt, saying, "Have you had an encouraging day, Bill?"

"Nope. Nothing has gone right today."

"Well, perhaps it's time things turned around. This may be the greatest day of your entire life!"

"What do you mean?"

"Well, Jesus Christ died for you so that you could be freed from all sin and guilt, have peace and joy in your life every day, and live in heaven with Him for all eternity. That's pretty encouraging news. It's made all the difference in my life. Would you like to receive Him into your life?"

"I dunno. What do I have to do?"

"Just ask Him to come into your life and be your Savior and Lord. You can do that very simply. Just say, 'Lord Jesus Christ, I know I need You. Have mercy on me, a sinner. Please forgive me of my sins and come into my heart and make me a new person. I need the joy and peace You alone can give me.' You'd like to experience that, wouldn't you, Bill?"

"Yeah, I would."

"Well, we can pray right now." (You've noticed that there's still nobody else in the store.)

"I don't know how to pray."

"Oh, that's okay. I'll pray, and you just repeat after me."

You lead Bill in a short prayer. You go on to share with him in about three sentences that in order for him to grow as a new creation in Christ, he needs to get involved with a fellowship of believers where he'll hear and learn the Word of God, get a Bible and read it every day, and talk to the Lord daily. "You can even do that here in the store, at times like this, when there's nobody around."

Bill is beaming. Without a doubt, you're the finest customer he's ever had come into the store.

You're beaming, too! Another soul has been added to the Lord's kingdom.

Were you led by the Spirit?

Absolutely!

You continue on your way home, convinced that God answers prayer and directs your steps.

Approach or Avoid

When people are resisting God and hiding from the truth of God's Word, they'll literally run away from Him. The gospel produces a reaction from every person—either openness and receptivity or hardness and rejection.

One day, I spotted a man on a subway who was reading a Bible. "Pretty good Book you're reading," I said.

"Yes, it's the best," he replied. I asked him to read aloud a favorite Scripture, and as he did, I noticed a young woman who had been sitting nearby jump up suddenly and move away quickly—just far enough away to be out of hearing distance. It was interesting to see her obvious indignation as the man read Scripture.

We need to face the fact that...

Most People Aren't Ready to Receive

I wrote earlier that most people in the world today are not ready to receive Jesus. Many are. But the majority are not.

It's important that you face that fact and come to grips with it, or you will often feel a sense of disappointment, frustration, failure, and rejection when sharing your faith. The majority of the people I have talked to through the years have *not* received Jesus Christ. The fact is that most of the people with whom Jesus had contact during His ministry on this earth did not follow Him.

The Scriptures say that even after hearing Him speak and seeing His miracles, *"many of His disciples went back and walked with Him no more"* (John 6:66). Jesus Himself said, *"There are some of you who do not believe,"* and *"No one can come to Me unless it has been granted to him by My Father,"* and *"No one can come to Me unless the Father who sent Me draws him"* (John 6:64–65, 44).

Mathematically speaking, the Lord probably gets turned down three times out of four. The Scripture teaches that *"wide is the gate and broad is the way that leads to destruction, and there are many who go in by it. Because narrow is the gate and difficult is the way which leads to life, and there are few who find it"* (Matthew 7:13–14).

The important point, however, is to focus on that one person in four who is open and responsive to Him.

Furthermore, you aren't the one who prepares a heart to know the Lord. You are simply the one who does the harvesting—bringing the person to Christ and an opportunity to open his life to the Lord.

Let me remind you again of Jesus' words to His disciples: *"The harvest truly is great, but the laborers are few; therefore pray the Lord of the harvest to send out laborers into His harvest"* (Luke 10:2).

It is the Lord who, through His Holy Spirit, speaks to people's hearts. It is the Lord who allows the seed of the gospel to take root deep within the soul of a human being and there begin to grow to the point of harvest. It is the Lord who brings a person to new birth in His own time so that the person might be born anew, healthy, and rightly fitted for a divine purpose. Yes, it is the Lord who is the vinedresser (see John 15:1–2) and the author and finisher of our faith (see Hebrews 12:2).

Don't Judge the Soil but Sow the Good Seed

Again, your job is to sow the good seed of God's Word. You know that the seed is good if it's the Word of God. I like the way the *Amplified Bible* describes the Word of God:

> *For the Word that God speaks is alive and full of power [making it active, operative, energizing, and effective]…exposing and sifting and analyzing and judging the very thoughts and purposes of the heart.*
> (Hebrews 4:12)

Those same descriptive words relate to a living seed. A seed presents a challenge to the soil. And if the soil is ready—if it is moist enough, fertile enough, and exposed to enough sunlight—the soil will allow that seed to germinate, take root, and grow. If the soil is too hard, too rocky, too cold, or too dry, the seed will lie dormant.

Your job is not to judge the soil but to sow the good seed.

Recall that this was the message of the parable that Jesus told about a sower who went out and sowed seeds. Some fell on hard ground, some grew up in thorny ground, some couldn't sprout because of the rocks in the soil. But that which fell on good soil sprang up and bore fruit—thirtyfold, sixtyfold, even a hundredfold. (See Matthew 13:3–9, 18–23.)

You can't always tell what kind of soil lies under the crusty outer countenance of a person. You can't tell how dry or stony his inner heart may be. You can't tell how much the Son has already warmed his heart. That, however, isn't really your job. Your job is to sow seed.

> THE SEED—THE WORD OF GOD, THE NAME OF JESUS, THE TELLING OF THE GOSPEL—WILL TEST THE SOIL.

The seed—the Word of God, the name of Jesus, the telling of the gospel—will test the soil.

The apostle Paul said, *"I planted, Apollos watered, but God gave the increase. So then neither he who plants is anything, nor he who waters, but God who gives the increase"* (1 Corinthians 3:6–7).

Pass It On—Freely

In Matthew 10:8, Jesus said, *"Freely you have received, freely give."*

What have you received?

The abundance of grace. The gift of righteousness. The provision of God to reign in life through the One, Jesus Christ. (See Romans 5:17.) These are just a few of the many things that have been given to you as free gifts. You received them by faith in Jesus Christ, who gave them to you. Now it is your joy to give them by faith to others.

The Holy Spirit will enable you to do it!

Questions for Reflection and/or Discussion

1. What are some ways we can know if God has prepared a person's heart to receive our witness?

2. What is the most effective strategy in bringing others to Christ?

3. Why is it important that we not judge by outward appearances?

4. How can you become a more spiritually discerning person?

5. Give some examples of how you have experienced guidance in ministry or in sharing Christ.

6. What do we learn from Jesus' parable of the sower about people's responses to the Word of God?

7. What should be our response when people resist the message of Christ?

$-10-$

MINISTRY OF RECONCILIATION

Sharing the Lord Jesus with others is a ministry of reconciliation. Salvation brings a person to a point where he is truly reconciled to the Father.

The apostle Paul wrote,

All things are of God, who has reconciled us to Himself through Jesus Christ, and has given us the ministry of reconciliation, that is, that God was in Christ reconciling the world to Himself, not imputing their trespasses to them, and has committed to us the word of reconciliation. (2 Corinthians 5:18–19)

As we seek to reconcile people to the Father, we must remember that many people will be resistant to the gospel of Christ, for various reasons. Although God, through the work of Christ, does not count our sins against us, Satan leads many people to believe that something is wrong with them that God can't change. The fact is that we, as unregenerate human beings, were all under Satan's influence and bondage. We were under false ownership and bad management.

The good news is that the Lord Jesus Christ came to save and transform us, regardless of how badly we may be broken, bruised, or battered. Jesus came to bring about a transfer of ownership and new management— His management by the Holy Spirit. He gives us His Spirit not only to correct the previous abuse in our lives and to cover it with His love, but also to make us new creations in His image and likeness so that we can live and operate as Jesus did when He was on the earth.

127

Jesus came to seek and to save the lost, heal the brokenhearted, bring recovery, and preach good news to the poor of spirit. (See Luke 19:10; 4:18.) Our mission is His mission!

The words we speak to another person must be words that build up, lead forward, and promote reconciliation.

Salvation Is More than Avoiding Hell and Going to Heaven

The ministry of reconciliation is one that we can offer both believers and nonbelievers. Salvation involves so much more than avoiding hell or eternal damnation. Many people's understanding of salvation is limited to their being forgiven for their sins and going to heaven when they die. In other words, they believe their past is covered and their future is secure. But their present is filled with defeat, frustration, and a lack of fruitfulness.

The fullness of salvation means being restored to a relationship with our Creator God. It is Christ now living in us! It is knowing Him and walking in the power of the Holy Spirit. It is sharing the very life of God here on earth, on the way to heaven.

To put it in theological terms, we have been justified, we are being sanctified, and, one day, we will be glorified, all because of the salvation we have in Christ. That means we are saved from the penalty of sin and the power of sin; and, one day in the future, we will be saved from the very presence of sin. The finished work of Christ on the cross has made full provision for our past, present, and future.

THE GOOD THINGS PROVIDED FOR US IN CHRIST ARE SO WONDERFUL, WHY WOULD WE WANT TO KEEP THEM TO OURSELVES?

An adequate understanding of the wonderful salvation we have in Him is cause for great joy and rejoicing. Peace that passes all understanding and joy unspeakable are ways the apostles described it. (See Philippians 4:7 KJV; 1 Peter 1:8 KJV.)

The good things that the Lord has provided for us in Christ are so wonderful and compelling, why would we want to keep them to ourselves?

Here, then, are ways in which we can be effective ministers of reconciliation.

Be Flexible in Your Approach

First, as I noted briefly in an earlier chapter, we should recognize that the ministry of reconciliation can take on many forms of expression.

Some people respond well to a straightforward approach. They like simple, direct questions. They respond simply and directly.

Others need time to engage in a relationship—to exchange pleasant comments, to explore ideas and ask questions, to share.

Be sensitive to both types of people, and adjust your methods to them. I make every effort not to...

+ make demands, either in my tone of voice or in the words I use.

+ put people on the spot.

+ place any more burden of guilt upon people than they are already feeling.

+ embarrass people.

It is important to maintain eye contact. Listen. Bring the conversation to a close with a positive word about Jesus or a prayer (even if the person chooses not to receive Him into his life). I try to state as much of the gospel message and the Word of God as I can in the time available.

Keep the door open for any future dialogue. Seek to cultivate a relationship for an ongoing witness and spiritual influence.

Avoid Arguments

Second, it's important to avoid arguments with people.

What do you do if the person says he doesn't believe the Bible?

I don't spend a lot of time on apologetics—arguing the truth of God's Word. God's Word is true, and we can know that fact only by experience as the Holy Spirit imprints it on our hearts and as we see that the truth of the Bible works as we live out its promises and precepts.

Jesus asked His disciples, *"Who do men say that I, the Son of Man, am?"* (Matthew 16:13). He then followed up their answer with another question: *"Who do you say that I am?"* (verse 15). Peter responded, *"You are the Christ, the Son of the living God"* (verse 16). And Jesus said, *"Blessed are you, Simon Bar-Jonah, for flesh and blood has not revealed this to you, but My Father who is in heaven"* (verse 17). The truth about Jesus is a revelation from the Father. This is the case about everything Jesus said and did in the Bible, and for every aspect of the Old Testament that points to Jesus and that Jesus fulfilled.

You cannot convince someone else that God's Word is true. Your heavenly Father must do that.

You can teach people what you know of God's Word, if they are interested in hearing it.

You can pray for them.

> YOU CAN GIVE A PERSONAL WITNESS TO THE TRUTH OF THE BIBLE WITHOUT ENTERING INTO DEBATES ON CERTAIN VERSES OR PASSAGES.

And you can simply say to those who protest against the Bible in their hearts and claim they don't believe it, "I believe the Bible *is* true. I base my belief on what it's meant in my life and on how I've seen it work in the lives of others I know who believe and obey its teaching." There is a great deal of difference between mental assent and experiential knowledge. In other words, you can give a personal witness to the truth of the Bible without entering into debates on certain verses or passages.

Avoid arguments as much as possible, because…

+ Most arguments are simply a diversion. Often, the person is trying to avoid the real truth about Jesus Christ by calling into question a passage of Scripture. Recognize the diversion for what it is—an attempt to sidestep the truth. Bring the conversation back to Jesus Christ and the centrality of the cross. Keep it focused there.

+ Most arguments aren't resolved. The person who argues about a verse of Scripture is not likely to be convinced by you. He usually has adopted a deeply entrenched position about that verse of Scripture, and he isn't going to let go of it easily. Trust the Holy Spirit to continue working in his life and to soften his position so that someday he might come to know the Lord.

Even if you win an argument, you'll likely lose the opportunity to introduce that person to a relationship with Christ.

I'm speaking, of course, about arguments based on doctrinal issues. You certainly can respond to a person's negative statements.

There are many exceptions to this approach. When you sense that a person has a genuine question or concern, you deal with it.

For example, I dealt with a man years ago who was a highly technical thinker with a scientific education. He expressed doubts about how God could use the stars to lead the wise men and had questions about heaven.

I continued to dialogue with him and even went to a Christian bookstore and bought a book for him that dealt with those issues. As a result of our ongoing relationship and my continuing to share with him, he came to Christ in a matter of a few months. Incidentally, this man later became a pastor.

Instead of Arguing, Reason and Persuade

The Scriptures say, "'*Come now, and let us reason together,*' *says the Lord*" (Isaiah 1:18). Reasoning together is not arguing. An argument is a combative conversation in which sides are taken, positions are drawn, and evidence is put forth to pull a person across an imaginary line in the philosophical sands.

Reasoning together is an entirely scriptural activity to undertake. It is usually an activity for believers—searching the Scriptures for assurance, edification, and strength.

Acts 28:23 says that Paul received people into his lodging on an appointed day, and "*he explained and solemnly testified of the kingdom of God, persuading them concerning Jesus from both the Law of Moses and the Prophets, from morning till evening.*" Persuasion can be an act of wooing others toward Jesus Christ. We are called to persuade. The apostle Paul openly declared to the Corinthians, "*We persuade men*" (2 Corinthians 5:11).

Just as reasoning is not arguing, persuasion is not an argument. To be persuaded, a person must have opened his mind to some degree toward the gospel, and he must have put himself into a position of being willing to hear. Even King Agrippa had that stance as he heard Paul's defense. He said, *"You almost persuade me to become a Christian"* (Acts 26:28). Agrippa's encounter with Paul was not one marked by argument. It was one in which he heard Paul out.

I do not find a place in the Scriptures where argument is encouraged or where it results in people coming to Christ. Argumentation is combative. It polarizes. It further entrenches the lost person into a position that he becomes determined to defend.

> I WOULD RATHER WALK AWAY FROM ARGUMENT AND LEAVE THE PERSON WITH A POSITIVE, AUTHORITATIVE WORD FROM THE LORD SPOKEN IN PEACE THAN ENGAGE IN A VERBAL OR DOCTRINAL FISTFIGHT.

I would rather walk away from argument and leave the person with a positive, authoritative word from the Lord spoken in peace than engage in a verbal or doctrinal fistfight that results in all parties being bruised. There are too many people ready to respond to the Lord for us to spend time engaged in something that may further alienate a person from Him.

To avoid arguments, of course, is also to avoid those issues that are so often divisive in witnessing encounters. I rarely discuss controversial political issues with people. I turn conversations away from controversial or divisive issues and toward Christ, the cross, and God's love. In a ministry or witnessing situation, I try to avoid giving an opinion about anything that doesn't relate directly to the Lord Jesus and how He can meet that person's need.

Avoid Questions That Have No Answer

You will seldom be able to explain certain issues to the satisfaction of another person. Their answers simply do not lie on this side of eternity. Suffering is one of those issues. Rejection by loved ones is another. You can spend hours trying to find an answer or an idea that satisfies the person, but, generally, those hours are spent without reaching a definitive conclusion or reaching an answer that is watertight.

Rather than attempt to explain what I do not understand about God, I attempt to turn a conversation toward truths I do have some degree of understanding of and experience in:

+ God loves. (See, for example, John 3:16.)

+ God cares. (See, for example, 1 Peter 5:7.)

+ God heals and makes whole. (See, for example, James 5:15–16.)

+ God forgives and cleanses us from sin and guilt. (See, for example, 1 John 1:7.)

+ God restores and raises anew. (See, for example, 2 Corinthians 1:9–10.)

+ God gives eternal life. (See, for example, 1 John 5:11.)

The entire ministry of Jesus on earth was a demonstration of all these actions and attributes.

Stay focused on the person and work of Christ. Stay focused on what you do know about the Lord—that He desires, above all, that all people should come to know Him, receive Him, trust Him, and abide in Him, even as He abides in them.

In his book *Mere Christianity*, C. S. Lewis wrote,

Ever since I became a Christian I have thought that the best, perhaps the only, service I could do for my unbelieving neighbours was to explain and defend the belief that has been common to nearly all Christians at all times.[1]

Sticking with the central themes of the Christian faith will keep us from being sidetracked onto secondary or fringe issues.

Ask the Right Questions to Get the Right Answer

I rarely ask a person, "Are you a Christian?"

Many people equate Christianity with church membership. Some people assume that if they were baptized as children or born into Christian families, they are Christians.

Others come to the conclusion that they are Christians through a process of elimination: "Well, I'm not a Hindu, I'm not a Buddhist, I'm not a Muslim, I'm not Jewish, I'm not an atheist, so I must be a Christian." Still others have heard that the United States is a "Christian nation," so they assume that because they are citizens of the United States, they are Christians.

Neither church membership, nor infant baptism, nor a personal philosophy, nor general citizenship is the same as having a personal relationship with the Lord Jesus Christ, being filled with His Holy Spirit, and having an assurance that your sins have been forgiven and that your eternal home will be in heaven with the Lord.

I also avoid asking, "Are you born again?" without some explanation.

Some people have many definitions for that phrase, and they may say yes for the wrong reasons, or they may say no, even though they have received Jesus Christ into their lives!

Instead of asking people an "Are you _____?" type of question, I prefer to present the gospel message first and then ask them to respond to it.

> INSTEAD OF ASKING, "WOULD YOU LIKE TO BECOME A CHRISTIAN?" ASK, "WOULD YOU LIKE TO RECEIVE THE LORD JESUS INTO YOUR LIFE?"

If I must use a question in leading a person to the point of decision, I do not say, "Would you like to become a Christian?" Instead, I ask, "Would you like to receive the Lord Jesus Christ into your life?"

For example, as I wrote about earlier, I once struck up a conversation with a young man who was setting up for a breakfast meeting at which I was scheduled to speak. I arrived early for a time of prayer and preparation in the banquet hall, and he was supervising the staff as they set up the tables for the guests.

After a few casual comments with this young man, I said, "I'm scheduled to be on the program today. Would you mind if I rehearsed with you a little of what I'm planning to say?"

He said, "Sure, go ahead."

I said, "I'm going to be sharing today about the Lord Jesus Christ and what it means that He died on the cross for our sins." I went on to give him a paragraph or two of summary about who Jesus is and how to receive the Lord.

I then asked him, "Have you ever received the Lord?"

He said he hadn't. I said, "You'd like to be forgiven of your sins and know you have everlasting life, though, wouldn't you?"

He said he would. We prayed together, and as we finished, the people began to arrive for the breakfast, so we went our separate ways.

I mentioned previously that during my presentation to the group, I started to share about praying with the young man, saying, "Let me tell you what happened earlier this morning." Just at that moment, he entered the banquet room and assumed that I had just introduced him. He came forward and gave his own testimony about what had happened to him. Praise God for those who experience a new birth and are so willing and eager to share their newfound faith!

Get to the Real Issues

Occasionally, you'll encounter somebody who will respond to you with a statement such as this: "I think I've done this," or "Well, I was baptized as a child. Is that what you mean?"

The person who questions or has doubts about his salvation usually falls into one of two categories. Either he was baptized as a child or went through some religious ritual, or he needs assurance that his confession of faith was genuine.

I usually try to help the person to evaluate his experience. A person will often readily admit that the experience he had in the past didn't really make a difference in his life.

When you are in doubt about what to do in evaluating or discussing a person's past spiritual experiences, I suggest this principle: rather than try to figure out some past experience, begin with where he is today. If the person has been genuinely born again, he won't mind praying with you and sealing the fact. If he has not had a genuine encounter with the Lord, your prayer with him can resolve the issue.

Help People to Examine Their Faith

The apostle Paul wrote to the Corinthians,

Examine yourselves as to whether you are in the faith. Test yourselves. Do you not know yourselves, that Jesus Christ is in you?; unless indeed you are disqualified. (2 Corinthians 13:5)

Let's recognize that some people have had a counterfeit conversion experience. They may have been convinced in their minds and stirred in their emotions, walked down the aisle, and made some decision. And yet, they walked away from that experience to continue to live a "disqualified" life. The experience brought about no real change of heart.

> SOME PEOPLE HAVE ACCEPTED THE HISTORICAL JESUS BUT HAVE NEVER ENCOUNTERED THE LIVING CHRIST.

That's what I call a psychological conversion. They have made up their minds about Jesus, but their spirits have not been regenerated. They have accepted the historical Jesus but have never encountered the living Christ.

As you share the gospel with a person, he will generally make a statement about what his experience has been. He'll not only express it to you, but, in so doing, he'll also see his past action more clearly for what it was.

Don't leave a person wondering if a past experience qualifies him for eternal life. Leave him with a present-day experience that assures him of the fact.

In seeking to help a person determine his true spiritual condition, it's often useful to ask, "If you were to die today, do you know for sure that you would go to heaven?" or "What are you depending on to get you into heaven?"

If the person's answer is anything other than Jesus Christ and His provision of salvation, you know he needs further spiritual guidance.

Take Dominion over Evil Spirits

A Conflict between Two Kingdoms

Jesus Christ conquered sin, death, and hell on the cross, and He destroyed Satan's power and control over our lives.

Most people don't realize that they are operating under one of two influences: the influence of the Holy Spirit or the influence of unholy spirits. Most people think they're "doing their own thing" when they aren't following God. The truth is that they are doing Satan's bidding and don't know it. They are slaves to a master they haven't yet acknowledged.

A person is under the dominion of either Satan or the Lord. The Bible speaks of only two kingdoms: one of light, ruled by the Lord Jesus Christ, and the other of darkness, ruled by the fallen Lucifer and his demonic minions.

Satan specializes in misusing, abusing, and prostituting our humanity. He does an extreme job on some people, more so than on others. But all of us are victims, to some extent, of "child abuse." As children of God, we've all been victims of the devil's attacks and abuse at some point in our lives.

Certainly, in our unregenerate, lost condition before coming to Christ, we were of our father the devil (see John 8:44) and were abused by him without even realizing it.

Jesus Destroyed the Devil's Authority

Jesus destroyed the devil's authority over mankind. (See, for example, Hebrews 2:14–15.) When we align ourselves with the Lord Jesus—through an act of our wills in choosing to repent of our sins, receiving Jesus into our lives, and making a choice to follow Him and be filled with and guided by His Spirit—the devil no longer has a right to us. The devil may try to exert his influence over us, but it's now our privilege in Christ to resist him. The Bible tells us, *"Submit to God. Resist the devil and he will flee from you"* (James 4:7).

Notice that the previous verse says, *"God resists the proud, but gives grace to the humble"* (verse 6).

Scripture goes on to say, *"Submit to God."* It's only after we have submitted to God that we are able to resist the devil.

We have absolute victory over the devil through our risen, indwelling Lord. *"He who is in you is greater than he who is in the world"* (1 John 4:4).

You Can Be Victorious over the Devil's Deceptive Strategies

Our role after our spiritual new births is to be people who reign, who triumph, who win, who are victorious over the deceptive methods and strategies of the devil.

We no longer need to be dominated by our circumstances; by the world, the flesh, and the devil. That doesn't mean that we will be forever in a state of happiness, wealth, and health. It does mean that no matter in what situation we find ourselves, we can have an inner stability that endures. Our faith can remain steadfast, as 1 Peter 5:8–9 so vividly describes: *"Your adversary the devil walks about like a roaring lion, seeking whom he may devour. Resist him, steadfast in the faith."*

Furthermore, we—through the power of the Holy Spirit—have authority over evil spirits. The only thing the devil has left is a lie—a "roar."

SATAN HAS NO POWER OVER THE BELIEVER WHO KNOWS AND EXERCISES HIS AUTHORITY IN CHRIST.

Satan can come roaring as a lion—with a lying roar, but he isn't a lion. He pretends to be a real lion with power, when, actually, his power was stripped from him by the Lord Jesus. Only Jesus is the reigning Lion of Judah.

Satan is a defeated foe. He is a deceiver and a usurper, but he has no power over the believer in Christ who knows and exercises his authority in Christ.

You Have Been Given the Power to Back Up the Command

The Scriptures say, *"Be not deceived."* (See, for example, Galatians 6:7 KJV.) Don't give in to fear at the devil's roar! Don't be tricked by just a roar.

Jesus promised,

All authority has been given to Me in heaven and on earth. Go therefore and make disciples of all the nations, baptizing them in the name of the

*Father and of the Son and of the Holy Spirit, teaching them to observe
all things that I have commanded you; and lo, I am with you always,
even to the end of the age.*　　　　　　　　(Matthew 28:18–20)

Again, God's Word says, "*He* [the Holy Spirit] *who is in you is greater
than he* [the enemy of your souls] *who is in the world*" (1 John 4:4).

Jesus doesn't ask you to do something that He doesn't equip you with
power to do. Read Acts 1:8 again: "*You shall receive power when the Holy
Spirit has come upon you; and you shall be witnesses to Me.*"

How do you take dominion over the enemy of your souls when he
comes roaring at you? By faith. Resist the devil's roar. Stand firm in your
resolve that Jesus is Lord and will forever be Lord, and that, therefore, He
is Lord over the situation confronting you right now.

The authority that was given to Jesus has been given to us.

From time to time, you will encounter those who are held in bondage
by the devil's roar. Generally speaking, these are people who exhibit a great
deal of fear. It's as if they are paralyzed by the devil's lie. Take action to
release them from that paralysis.

A Prayer for Release from Fear's Bondage

There will be times when you'll engage in a conversation with a person
who will seem interested in what you are saying but who will exhibit a fear
of receiving the Lord. He might say such things as "I'd like to accept the
Lord, but..." or "I want to do this, but..." or "This makes sense to me, but
I just don't know...."

Take authority over that excuse. Ask the person immediately, "Why
don't you let me pray about that—that you'll have the freedom to receive
the Lord Jesus?" And then pray,

Heavenly Father, I ask You to free [the person's name], in the name
of Jesus, from any thoughts or plaguing doubts that are keeping
him from trusting and receiving Your Son, the Lord Jesus Christ,
into his heart as his personal Savior and Lord.

Some people are held in the bondage by a decades-old hurt from child-
hood, a plaguing memory, a deep-seated doubt, or an indefinable fear.

Recognize these situations for the spiritual battles that they are. Take authority. Ask the Holy Spirit to do the releasing in their spirits. Use the name of Jesus with confidence.

After you've prayed with a person, ask again, "Do you feel you can now receive the Lord Jesus into your life?" In my experience, I've found that in many cases the person says yes.

People who say, "I'd like to" or "I want to" are just one step away from saying, "I will." Help them to take that final step!

Years ago, I led a lady to Christ who had been in great spiritual bondage. I shared with her after a church service one night and explained the gospel to her. She admitted that she knew she needed to be saved and went on to say she wanted to receive Christ, but then added, "Something is just holding me back."

I asked her if I could pray for her, and she said that would be fine. So, I prayed and took authority over all the powers of darkness in her life, in the name of Jesus.

Afterward, I explained further how Jesus Christ's death on the cross and His resurrected life had made provision for her to be set free and delivered from Satan.

We then prayed together, and she was able to open up and call on the Lord for salvation and deliverance.

EVERY SPIRITUAL NEW BIRTH IS A SUPERNATURAL WORK OF THE HOLY SPIRIT, REGARDLESS OF THE DEGREE OF SPIRITUAL BLINDNESS.

Actually, every spiritual new birth is a supernatural work of the Holy Spirit, regardless of the degree of spiritual blindness and bondage a person is under. Some are just more intensely bound than others.

Keep in mind that Jesus Christ is Lord of all. He is King of Kings and Lord of Lords, and we have victory through Him and authority to set the captives free. Also remember that all that Jesus is, He is in you; and all that He is in you, He is prepared to be through you.

Questions for Reflection and/or Discussion

1. What is the key factor in people experiencing spiritual transformation?

2. What is the ministry of reconciliation?

3. How does being flexible help in relating the gospel to others?

4. What are some simple ways of avoiding arguments with people when sharing about life in Christ?

5. Discuss the role of reasoning and persuading in sharing our faith.

6. What are some right and wrong questions to ask people when witnessing?

7. How can you help a person to be sure about his or her relationship with Christ?

8. Discuss the spiritual and supernatural in relation to experiencing freedom and bondage.

9. On what basis do you know that you can take authority over and have victory over evil forces that seek to prevent people from coming to Christ?

—11—

Seizing the Moment

Every salesperson knows that the most important part of any deal is "the close." The sale representative can get an appointment with a prospective buyer, give his presentation, and answer all the questions asked about the product. Yet, if he never asks the customer to buy, the presentation has no point. The appointment bears no fruit.

A good negotiator also knows he must bring closure to a proposition. Every effective teacher or preacher will seek to bring people to a point of acting on the message he presents.

After I've shared the gospel with a person and sense that he is ready to respond, I seek to bring him to a point of decision, a point of opening his life to the Lord.

> WHEN YOU'VE SHARED THE GOSPEL WITH SOMEONE AND SENSE HIS READINESS, SEEK TO BRING HIM TO A POINT OF DECISION TO TRUST CHRIST.

I've found that the best way to do that is to ask something like, "Are you ready to trust Christ now?" Or, I might say, "Let me lead us in prayer, and you can respond to the Lord right now."

Give the Person an Opportunity

Remember, it's not your responsibility to convince a person to receive Jesus. It's your responsibility only to give him an opportunity.

If you don't give people an opportunity, they most likely won't respond. If you do give them an opportunity, it's up to them how they will respond.

Their response is directly related to what the Holy Spirit is doing in their lives.

Different Facets, but the Same Basics

The basics of the "spiritual new birth," or receiving Christ, are the same for each person, even though each individual will experience it in a way unique to him. That's true in natural birth, also. Women and their physicians have noted time and time again, "Each pregnancy is different." The point is, each baby is different. And yet, each baby is born in pretty much the same way. Intense contractions result in a baby being pushed through the birth canal and into a new world, followed by a separation from his mother as the umbilical cord is cut. A gasp or cry comes from the baby as he begins to breathe on his own, and an eager desire for nourishment soon follows. There are slight variations on that theme, of course, but the natural flow of birthing events is consistent, even though individual differences may keep doctors on their toes or put nurses into near-frantic motion.

The birthing analogy is one Jesus Himself used in describing what happens to a person when he is spiritually renewed by the Holy Spirit. (See John 3:1–8.) Each person is unique, and the events leading up to that person's spiritual birth are unique. Yet the process of his birthing is similar to that experienced by all others who have received Christ.

Birthing in our world today can come either by natural means or through a cesarean section. Birthing spiritually also happens generally by two methods: petitioning or confessing.

Petitioning and Confessing

Petitioning the Lord

In petitioning, which we usually think of as prayer, the person is *asking* the Lord to do a work in his life. In confessing, the person is *acknowledging* the work that the Lord is doing. Both methods arrive at the same point: accepting what the Lord has done and receiving Him into one's life.

Both a prayer and a petition need to cover essentially the same points:

- ◆ Acknowledgment that Jesus Christ is the Son of God who died on the cross for our sins, as our substitute.

- ◆ Acknowledgment of one's sinfulness and need for the Lord, and a willingness to turn to Him and from the self-life.

- ◆ Acknowledgment that Jesus Christ rose from the dead to give us eternal life.

- ◆ Acknowledgment by faith that Jesus Christ has forgiven us for our sins.

- ◆ Acknowledgment that we are willing to receive Christ into our lives.

God's Word teaches us that we believe and then receive. (See, for example, Acts 10:43.) A prayer or a confession needs to put a person in a position where he says, "I believe the gospel to be true. I receive Christ into my life."

The exact words used in a "sinner's prayer" or in a confession can vary. God is most interested in the heart and in a willful surrender to Him.

Most assuredly, the time of prayer does not need to be long. I have often led a person into a spiritual birth experience with a prayer as short as this:

> GOD IS MOST INTERESTED IN THE HEART AND IN A WILLFUL SURRENDER TO HIM.

Lord Jesus Christ, I know I need You. Have mercy upon me, a sinner. Save me. Come into my life and make me a new person. I now turn from my sinful ways and trust You to forgive me of my sins, fill me with Your Spirit, and make me the kind of person You want me to be. In Jesus' name, amen.

Can Such a Simple Time of Prayer Work?

I believe that the moment a person repents of his sins, receives Jesus Christ into his life, and receives God's forgiveness, his eternal destiny is changed; he has a home in heaven, and he is spiritually born into God's kingdom.

That's the promise made by our Lord Himself in the most famous of all Bible verses: *"For God so loved the world that He gave His only begotten Son, that whoever believes in Him should not perish but have everlasting life"* (John 3:16).

Jesus didn't say that person needed to complete a ten-week, new believers' class, or recite a long string of prayers or "I believe" statements, or bow *x* number of times toward a shrine, or make a pilgrimage to a holy place—or even down an aisle to an altar—in order to be born anew. He said that when we *believe* in Him—which involves turning our backs on our old, sinful ways and false beliefs, receiving forgiveness for those old ways and beliefs, and turning toward a new way of believing and a new life in the Lord—we have in that moment a new destiny.

Confessing Christ

THE BIBLE SAYS THAT "CONFESSING" JESUS IS LORD IS THE KEY TO SALVATION.

Many times, we believe that a person must bow his head, close his eyes, and pray a sinner's prayer in order to receive the Lord Jesus into his life. There's no place in the Bible where that traditional formula is set forth as necessary. What the Bible does say is that "confessing" Jesus is Lord is the key to salvation.

Once more, Romans 10:9–10, 13 are particularly effective verses to read or quote. I often explain from these verses what it means to confess, believe, and call on the Lord:

> *If you confess with your mouth the Lord Jesus and believe in your heart that God has raised Him from the dead, you will be saved. For with the heart one believes unto righteousness, and with the mouth confession is made unto salvation....For "whoever calls on the name of the LORD shall be saved."* (Romans 10:9–10, 13)

If you are engaged in street evangelism in a rough section of town, the last thing anybody is interested in doing is bowing his head and closing his eyes. I found it an amazing discovery the day I learned that a person could receive Jesus into his life with his eyes open and his head up.

One method I've used over the years in bringing a person to the point of decision is this: When I sense he is ready, I just say, "You know, the Lord is here with us right now. We can include Him in our conversation, and you can call upon Him."

Again, I often explain to people that they don't have to be in a church building or go through a long religious ritual to be saved; the important thing is that in their hearts they respond to the Lord. Assure them that God is present and will respond to their need as they call upon Him.

My objective when sharing Christ with a lost person is to bring him to acknowledge Jesus as Lord and confess his need of Him. The particular prayer a person prays is secondary to his heart confession.

Jesus promised, "*Whoever confesses Me before men, him I will also confess before My Father who is in heaven*" (Matthew 10:32).

Remember that God is more concerned about the attitude of one's heart than He is about the particular words that are spoken.

One Pastor's Experience

Once, a pastor was with me and two other men in a restaurant on a day when four waitresses came to know the Lord. Upon experiencing firsthand what it meant to be involved in leading others to Christ, he made a firm commitment that he was going to engage in sharing Christ at every possible opportunity. Here is what he later told me:

"The following Sunday after church, I was having lunch at a restaurant. A waitress walked up to our table and poured us a second cup of coffee. I said to her, 'You know, there's something encouraging that's happened to those of us at this table that you might be interested in knowing about. The Lord is at work in our lives. What is the Lord doing in your life?'

"She looked at me and said, 'Absolutely nothing, and I don't care to hear about it.'

"I thought to myself, *Wow, what a beginning!*

"Now, at this particular steak house, the same waitress never seems to come to your table twice, so I watched for the next person the Lord might bring across my path. Sure enough, in a few minutes, a different waitress came to check on the coffee level in our cups, and I shared a little with her. She said, 'Yes, I've accepted the Lord, but I just don't seem to have the time to do all the things I want to do—like go to church regularly or get involved with a group of Christians.'

"I said to her very gently, 'You know, you seem to need some encouragement today, and perhaps that's why the Lord sent us here.' I didn't take my eyes off her as I continued to share, 'You need to have the Word of God established firmly in your life.' I offered her the opportunity to fill out a card with her name and address so I could send her some more information about God's Word and invite her to attend our church.

"She took the card, filled it out, brought it back to me before we left, and seemed extremely grateful that the opportunity was before her to grow in the Lord. She had accepted the Lord into her life two years earlier, and she said I was the first person who had encouraged her walk with the Lord since that initial new-birth experience!"

How About an Opportunity to Reject?

The pastor continued his story:

"The next day, I drove into the gas station I usually frequent, and I saw the owner of the station standing inside. I felt convicted that I had never shared Christ with this man, even though I had seen him and talked to him dozens of times through the years. The service station owner knew I was a pastor and knew the name of the church where I served, and I knew his name. And yet, the name of Jesus had never been raised between us.

"This day, I felt the Holy Spirit prompting me to take a different tactic. I got out of my car, and, as I began to pump gas at the self-service pump, the service station owner came over to me. I greeted him warmly and then said, 'Doug, when are you finally going to turn your life over to the Lord Jesus Christ?'

"He stood there for a few minutes and then began to argue, raising first one objection and then another. I quietly kept pumping gas into my car, and then I responded, 'It's not the starving people in Africa, Doug. It's not the abused children. It's not the priest who rebuked you forty-five years ago. It's Jesus I'm talking to you about.' The man became silent.

"I said, 'You know, Doug, if you want to reject Jesus, I should also give you that opportunity today. If you accept Him, you accept Him and confess publicly as a part of being saved. But if you choose to reject Him, you should also reject Him publicly.'

"This put the situation in an entirely different light for this service station owner. He wasn't ready to say, 'I reject Jesus.' Instead, he responded, 'I'll think about it.'

"Why did I take that approach? Well, the thought came to me that someday I might pull into this service station and not find this man. Or, perhaps something would happen to me so that I never came to this service station again. How could I explain to the Lord that I had encountered a man several dozen times in my life and yet had never mentioned His name to him and had never given him an opportunity to accept or reject Jesus Christ?"

That is a good thought for each one of us to ponder as we recall the people whom we see again and again and again as we take clothes to be dry-cleaned, have our hair cut, take our shoes to be repaired, buy food at convenience stores, and so on. You know your routine. You know which people you see over and over.

- ✦ Consider your neighbors.
- ✦ Consider your children's teachers.
- ✦ Consider professionals you see on a regular basis.
- ✦ Consider your own family members.

Rejoicing with Grateful Hearts

People who come to the Lord may not know how to thank you. Sometimes, all they can do is smile. Sometimes, the emotions are too deep for words. Don't feel you need to linger in a conversation.

One cab driver said to me, "I woke up this morning with a lot of problems on my mind." I took his comment as an open door for sharing the gospel, and, during the course of the drive to my next appointment, he received Christ into his life. As we reached my destination and I started to get out of the cab, he said, "God sent you; I believe that! I feel a warmth inside me. He is doing something." I offered to send him a Bible, but he said, "I have one, and I'm going to start reading it tonight." As I attempted to pay the fare, he said, "This is on me. You've made this a special day."

GIVE A WORD OF ENCOURAGEMENT AND WORDS OF FOLLOW-UP OR REFERRAL WITH THE PERSON WHO HAS JUST RECEIVED CHRIST.

Rarely can a person express his thanks in a tangible way, and we shouldn't expect it. That's the only free cab ride I've ever received!

What we can do is rejoice with the person who has just received Christ. We can give a word of encouragement and words of follow-up or referral. (See chapter 13 for further discussion about follow-up.)

"God bless you and keep you" is a phrase that's been used by Christians for centuries as a parting expression. So is, "May the Lord make His face to shine upon you always." (See Numbers 6:24–25.) You'll find through experience the most comfortable "benediction" for you to use. Leave the person with a positive, uplifting word.

And If a Person Turns You Down...

+ Don't take it personally.

+ Don't let it discourage you.

+ Don't let it keep you from speaking of Jesus to someone else.

+ Do take it as a sign from the Lord about what He would have you do for that person: *Pray!*

 a. Pray that the Holy Spirit would bind the forces of spiritual darkness that are keeping that person blind to the truth.

 b. Pray that the Holy Spirit would have dominion over the enemy that is keeping him deaf, spiritually speaking, to the message of the gospel.

 c. Pray that the Holy Spirit might take authority over the principalities and powers that are keeping this person imprisoned and shut away in dungeons of despair, and that the Holy Spirit would bring into the person's life those who might lead him to God's light.

Again, leave the person with a positive word. "May you come to know Him someday" is one phrase you might use. Or, perhaps, "God loves you."

Let the last words the person hears from you be words that are filled with the Lord's kindness and mercy—whether he accepts or rejects the Lord.

Questions for Reflection and/or Discussion

1. Why is it important to encourage people to respond to or to act on the message of Christ?

2. Discuss what it means to be born again.

3. Where and when can someone respond to the grace of God?

4. What are the roles of believing and confessing in the spiritual new birth?

5. Give some examples of how you can connect with people who need the Lord.

—12—

TEAMWORK

The more you engage in sharing your life in Christ, the more you will find yourself telling others about your experiences. The great joy of leading a person to Christ is something you will want to share with fellow believers.

As you share with others the results of your ministry activities, and as they hear you giving the credit to the Lord for preparing hearts and changing lives, they'll be encouraged to be bolder in their witnessing. A desire to be active in sharing Christ will be stirred within them.

As they actively share their faith and see lives transformed, still other believers will be encouraged and emboldened.

When you become part of a support group of people who not only take sharing the gospel seriously, but who also are committed to engaging in witnessing at every opportunity, you'll find that you'll draw strength and boldness from that association.

> YOU WILL DRAW STRENGTH FOR WITNESSING BY BEING PART OF A GROUP OF PEOPLE COMMITTED TO REGULARLY SHARING THE GOSPEL.

It is vital for you always to...

Stay in Fellowship with Other Believers

The Lord never called us to walk this path alone.

He redeemed us so that, together, we could be His "body," with each member fitted to the next so that the entire body can be whole. The Lord is the One who devised the means by which the Holy Spirit gives different gifts and abilities to different people for the building up of the whole. (See, for example, Ephesians 4:11–16; Romans 12:4–8.)

In your association with a group that is committed to sharing the gospel, you'll...

+ receive a great deal of insight as you learn new approaches to try.

+ gain strength from prayer times in which you join your hearts together in asking the Lord to prepare you and to prepare others for a spiritual new-birth experience.

+ have an opportunity to practice sharing your testimony with others.

If an active witness support group isn't available for you to join, prayerfully consider starting such a group within your church or Bible study group.

As your group's witness in your community becomes more widespread, you may find that you will meet a person who says, "You know, a man just told me about the Lord a few days ago." If the person has not received the Lord into his life, your witness is one more opportunity for him to do so. If he has, you have a prime opportunity to encourage him in the Lord.

We All Learn Best by Doing

You will discover that you learn more about witnessing and ministering to others by doing it than by reading books, attending seminars, or hearing lectures or sermons about it.

A man once asked me if he could go with me wherever I went for a few days to see if what I had taught at a conference on personal evangelism really worked. He wanted to see witnessing and sharing Christ in action. This man was a pastor, yet he knew he needed to be more intentional and effective in personal witness and ministry. He did go with me, and he learned how to become an active witness and to lead others to Christ in the process.

Advancing the Kingdom Is a Team Effort

Whether we realize it or not, we are part of a team effort when it comes to advancing the kingdom of God. Again, the leader of that team is Jesus Christ Himself. *"He is the head of the body, the church"* (Colossians 1:18).

When we have the opportunity to bring someone to faith in Christ, it's usually because someone else has already had an influence on that person's life. And others will be a part of his growth and maturity in the Lord.

So, we just enter into the labor and influences of a lot of other people in a person's life.

Teams Can Have Varied Approaches

The evangelism team you choose may be a short-term group gathered for a specific event. Over the years, I've had the joy of participating in many ministry projects, such as those that shared Christ at international sporting events, the Olympic Games, and other similar gatherings.

One of those ministry projects I was involved in was at the Olympic Summer Games in Los Angeles, California, in 1984. There was a special movement of God there, and a large number of people came to the Lord during the games.

The evangelism team members shared their life in Christ in ways that were varied and distinctive.

+ Children performed skits and sang songs about Jesus in nearby parks.
+ Drama troupes presented the gospel in pantomime.
+ A young man who was a former gang member told his story on street corners.

Each group, each subgroup, each team, each person presented Jesus in a unique way. It was a truly amazing phenomenon to watch as the Holy Spirit orchestrated this mass outreach to people from so many nations, both athletes and spectators.

The most amazing thing to me was that the purpose of their witness was the same—to share the gospel and to lead people to the Lord.

Later, I reflected on the thought that, from the Lord's vantage point in heaven, each day is a day of mobilizing His evangelism teams on this earth. Each day, the Holy Spirit holds an agenda of arranging unbelievers to cross the paths of believers. He speaks. He woos. He draws. He compels. He coordinates schedules, encounters, times, places, people, personalities, experiences, and backgrounds for one supreme purpose—to draw lost people to a relationship with Jesus Christ so that they might experience God's power in their lives now and live with the Lord forever.

> **FROM THE LORD'S VANTAGE POINT IN HEAVEN, EACH DAY IS A DAY OF MOBILIZING HIS EVANGELISM TEAMS ON THIS EARTH.**

If a large convention or group is coming to your city, make plans to mingle with the crowd. Only one thing can put a stop to the Lord's sovereign work in setting up appointments for life-changing witness encounters—our unwillingness to open our mouths and share the good news of Jesus Christ.

Expect to Be Built Up as a Body of Believers

When we witness to others about the Lord, we are not only sharing the gospel, bringing people into the kingdom, and planting seeds that the Holy Spirit can grow into an eternal harvest; no, still more is at work. The very process is transforming *us* into the likeness of Jesus.

Nothing makes you more like Jesus than demonstrating and sharing the love and grace of God with others.

It's through seeking to honor God and to bring His kingdom to earth that you put yourself in a position to do only what you see the Father doing, and to speak only what the Father compels you to speak—which is just the way Jesus said He lived. (See John 5:19; 8:38.)

Christ came to seek and to save the lost. He is now living in us to carry out that purpose.

God has given us a great privilege to take part in His divine activity of building up His kingdom.

Pray and Expect Results

Jesus promised His followers, *"He who believes in Me, the works that I do he will do also; and greater works than these he will do, because I go to My Father"* (John 14:12). How is that possible? It certainly isn't possible because of who we are. Rather, it's because Jesus fully expected to continue to live His life through us. He fully intended that we experience the same quality of life that He experienced on this earth. He said He was sending the Holy Spirit to indwell us for the purpose of assuring us that we could live in Him, even as He lives in us.

God delights in responding to biblically based, believing prayer. Pray for laborers, for boldness, for God to use you in advancing His kingdom. Then, expect God to answer your prayers! Indeed, the fields are *"white for harvest"* (John 4:35).

> GOD DELIGHTS IN RESPONDING TO BIBLICALLY BASED, BELIEVING PRAYER.

Remember that the early church prayed for boldness (see Acts 4:29), and that, in his letter to the Ephesians, the apostle Paul wrote, in effect, "Pray also for me, that the message may be given to me when I open my mouth to make known with boldness the mystery of the gospel." (See Ephesians 6:19.)

Certainly, if the apostle Paul and the disciples in the early church prayed for boldness, we also should pray for boldness to make known the love and truth of God.

I also believe there will be an increased openness to the gospel in the days ahead. We are living in difficult times, and I have observed that as people face personal difficulties, they seem to be more open to the Lord. In addition, as people hear about political, social, and economic problems in the nation and in the world, such as are reported by the news media on a regular basis, they tend to become more serious about spiritual things.

If we will ask God to do so, I believe He will…

+ increase our awareness of His greatness and His presence in our lives.

+ intensify our devotion to Him and His anointing on our lives.

+ expand our usefulness for the cause of Christ and the kingdom of God.

Our God is almighty, infinite, and unlimited. And He is willing and eager to pour out His blessings and power through each of us.

God does not show partiality; He desires to use each and every one of us.

Trust Him to respond to your prayers and expect Him to give you both boldness and gentleness to speak the truth in love. (See Ephesians 4:14–15.) Remember that your words, inspired by the Holy Spirit, have great power to touch hearts and change lives.

Questions for Reflection and/or Discussion

1. Discuss the importance of community and corporate witness in the body of Christ.

2. How does sharing your experiences with other believers encourage them to have more boldness in telling others about Christ?

3. How can a person's faith be contagious?

4. What is the value of teamwork in witnessing?

5. What does the process of witnessing do within *us*?

6. What does the *"greater works"* that Jesus talked about in John 14:12 mean to you?

7. What was Jesus referring to when He said that the fields are *"white for harvest"* (John 4:35)? How will you respond to His statement?

—13—

God's Follow-up Strategy

What a joy it is for us to know that we have been chosen by Christ and appointed so that we should go and bring forth fruit, and that our fruit should remain! (See John 15:16.)

God desires lasting and abiding fruit for His kingdom even more than we do. His plan and will is for every one of His followers to be a fruitful, victorious, and reproducing member of the body of Christ. Each of us has the capacity, by the indwelling presence of Christ, to bring others into the kingdom of God and to lead those new followers of His to become functioning, fruitful, and reproducing members of the body of Christ, also.

God Will Continue His Work

On a number of occasions, I've shared the gospel with a person, and he has not responded. Then, I've seen the person again several months later, and he has said, "You remember that you told me how to receive Christ?"

"Yes, I remember."

"Well, I did!"

The words shared with him—the good seed—finally germinated. The soil was finally ready for the seed, and what had been shared took root and grew.

God will not let people get away from what He has spoken to them.

Sometimes, I leave people who reject what I have to say with these parting words: "The Lord will be confirming to your heart what I've been telling you about His love for you and His desire to forgive you. You can respond to the Lord on your own. You don't need to pray with me or with anyone else. You can call upon the Lord wherever you are—even driving in your car or sitting in your home—and He'll hear you. The Bible promises, '*Whoever calls on the name of the LORD shall be saved.*' When you call upon Him, you can be assured that He'll hear you and respond to you." (See, for example, Romans 10:13.)

It is a great comfort to know that God will continue His work in the lives of those you share with. We don't always have to bring them to a point of decision or commitment, although we should when we can.

Tailor-Made Follow-up

Don't allow anyone to convince you that you shouldn't share the gospel with others just because you may not have an opportunity to follow up adequately or because they are not in your "church field."

Trust God to give you His creative, tailor-made follow-up and discipleship strategies, just as He gives you His creative, tailor-made approach to sharing Christ.

I make an effort to stay in touch and disciple, as much as possible, those whom I lead to faith in Christ. However, when I'm not able to personally follow up with them, I try to get their contact information. I then get them connected with a local church, a Bible study or prayer group, or a fellow believer who will stay in touch. It's important that a new follower of Christ connect with a group of people who are committed to Him and who have some life and vitality for the things of God.

> AS NEW BELIEVERS ARE EXPOSED TO OTHERS WHO ARE EXCITED ABOUT THE LORD AND ARE ACTIVELY SHARING THEIR FAITH, THEY WILL BE MORE LIKELY TO GROW IN CHRIST.

Again, it's just human nature that we become like the people we spend the most time with. So, as new believers are exposed to others who are excited about the Lord and are actively sharing their faith, they will be more likely to grow in Christ and to become healthy, productive members of the body of Christ.

When someone comes to Christ, and that person is literate and has access to Scripture, I like to suggest that he get started reading the Bible on a regular basis. A good place to begin is the gospel of John and the books of Colossians and 1 John. I also recommend a systematic plan of reading through the Bible every year. It takes only about fifteen minutes a day to read through the entire Bible in one year. If a person has difficulty reading, you might suggest that he listen to and/or view a copy of the Bible on CD, tape, or DVD.

Ideally, to get new believers off on the right track, I suggest that they get started with these basic spiritual disciplines:

1. Fellowship with other believers.

2. Read (or listen to) God's Word daily.

3. Spend time daily in prayer.

4. Share Christ with others.

You can share this simple 1-2-3-4 follow-up plan in a matter of minutes.

We trust the Holy Spirit to bring people to the point of being born anew. We must also trust the Holy Spirit to continue the process of spiritual growth. God is very good at watching over, protecting, and guiding His children.

The Scriptures are clear on this point. *"He who has begun a good work in you will complete it until the day of Jesus Christ"* (Philippians 1:6). The Holy Spirit will continue to develop a person throughout his lifetime. Just as our spiritual new birth comes about because of His wooing, so our growth continues as we submit our lives to His instruction.

Again, the Scriptures declare, *"He who calls you is faithful, who also will do it"* (1 Thessalonians 5:24). The Holy Spirit is the One who gently and persistently calls us toward the Lord Jesus. He is also the One who gives us the ongoing ability to remain true to our relationship with the Lord and to do all the things described in the verses preceding that statement: to be at peace, to follow good, to rejoice evermore, to pray without ceasing, to give thanks in everything, to quench not the Spirit, to despise not prophesying, to prove, or test, all things, to hold fast to that which is good, to abstain from all appearance of evil, and to come to the place where our whole spirit, soul, and body are preserved blameless unto the coming of the Lord Jesus Christ. (See 1 Thessalonians 5:11–23 KJV.) Your growth in Christ Jesus is something the Holy Spirit desires for you even more than you desire it for yourself.

Offer to Send a Bible

In addition to referring people to a place where they can receive pastoral care and the teaching of the Word, and encouraging them to read or listen to the Bible, you can also make an effort to personally provide them with a Bible or a New Testament.

> THE HOLY SPIRIT WILL USE THE SCRIPTURES TO GROW A NEW BELIEVER IN GRACE AND IN THE KNOWLEDGE OF THE LORD JESUS CHRIST.

If at all possible, I ask people if they'd be willing to give me their addresses so I can send them more information to help them in their walks with the Lord. You can usually purchase this material in bulk, at discounted prices, from ministries, from Bible societies, or through Christian bookstores.

One of the main reasons to encourage a new believer to get a Bible and read it is that the Holy Spirit will use the Scriptures to grow him in grace and in the knowledge of the Lord Jesus Christ and to reveal God's will to him.

Resources such as Christian books, tapes, CDs, videos, DVDs, Web sites, and podcasts; Christian radio and TV programs; and Bible study groups are all great assets in people's growth and walk with Christ. However, the Scriptures are the ultimate authority on who Jesus is, and nothing takes their place.

Use Bible Study Materials and the Gospel of John for Follow-up

In addition to volunteering to send a person a copy of the Bible or New Testament, I sometimes give them or tell them about Bible study materials and other resources.

I also often carry a supply of the gospel of John with me. In my opinion, the best follow-up literature you can give to a new believer is a copy of the complete gospel of John or the New Testament.

The gospel of John was written so that we *"may believe that Jesus is the Christ, the Son of God, and that believing* [we] *may have life in His name"* (John 20:31). Many times, when circumstances don't permit me to adequately share the gospel message, I like to give the person a gospel of John to read for himself. Many people have come to Christ just by reading the Word of God on their own.

A very effective approach I discovered years ago that has resulted in a number of people coming to Christ is to give someone a gospel of John and say, "Here's a book that was written by a man who knew Jesus personally, and it tells how you can know Him personally, as well."

> A VERY EFFECTIVE APPROACH IS TO GIVE SOMEONE A GOSPEL OF JOHN AND SAY, "HERE'S A BOOK THAT WAS WRITTEN BY A MAN WHO KNEW JESUS PERSONALLY, AND IT TELLS HOW YOU CAN KNOW HIM PERSONALLY, AS WELL."

That statement will often open up an opportunity to share the Lord right then. But if not, giving the person John's gospel is good seed sown and, many times, will result in follow-up opportunities.

God uses His Word in whatever form it is communicated. The spoken, written, or recorded Word continues to bear witness after the personal communication has ceased.

Check Out Local Churches That Present the Gospel in Other Languages

You may discover, as I have, that many people whom you lead to the Lord speak a language other than English. In recent years, I have found that a great many Spanish-speaking people are coming to know the Lord. There's a little-publicized, but very real, revival taking place among Spanish-speaking people across our land, and many are spiritually hungry and very open to the Lord. Following up with a New Testament translated into Spanish is important.

Over the years that my family and I have lived in the Houston area, I've had the joy of introducing people to Christ from all over the world. Many of them still have family and friends back in their home countries, some of whom have come to Christ as a result of their witness to them.

I shared the Lord with a man from Iran several years ago who later led his sister and brother-in-law to Christ over the telephone while they were still in Iran.

Within your own city, you may want to call upon, visit with, or at least gain basic information about some of the churches that present the gospel in other languages. Familiarize yourself with them so that you can refer new believers to them. Los Angeles, for example, is a city with a number of churches that regularly hold services in Chinese, Korean, Vietnamese, Spanish, and just about any other major language you can name. The same is true of New York City, Chicago, Houston, and other large cities. More and more, these cities are becoming cross-cultural mission fields. The Lord has literally brought the world to us.

Go Back for Repeated Visits

As I mentioned in an earlier chapter, as I have traveled to various cities over the years, I have always been on the lookout for people whom I've led to the Lord. I tend to stay in the same hotel in any given city, which provides me an opportunity to keep in touch and follow up personally with people, and also to introduce new people to the Lord by way of asking about those with whom I've shared in the past.

Similarly, once I've led a person to the Lord in a particular restaurant, I usually try to go back to that place as many times as I can during my stay in the city. I find that as one person in that group tells another, others become interested and are more ready to hear the gospel. The result is often a chain reaction.

I once returned to a restaurant where I had led two waitresses and a waiter to the Lord several months earlier. I said to my waitress, "I was here last October, and I had the opportunity to share with a couple of waitresses at that time who received Christ into their hearts. Do you know them, or do you know if they still work here?"

Most restaurants have a high turnover rate, and the waitress I asked didn't know the young women with whom I had shared the previous year. However, my question did open the door for me to say to my present waitress, "Their lives were dramatically changed that evening. They experienced a peace and joy they had never known before. By the way, have you received

Jesus Christ into *your* heart?" She hadn't. And, before I left that evening, she did pray with me to receive the Lord into her life.

The Impact of One Changed Life

Don't underestimate the power and impact of one changed life.

Again, when I am unable to adequately follow up on a new believer, I have confidence that the Lord will take care of His own. When we introduce people to Christ, and they enter into vital, personal relationships with the living God, we can count on the Holy Spirit's continuous work in their lives. (See Philippians 1:6.)

I take encouragement from the fact that one of the first deacons in the early church, Philip, didn't have a very long follow-up program with the Ethiopian eunuch he led to the Lord. Philip was led by the Holy Spirit to go to the Gaza desert and, upon seeing the Ethiopian in his chariot and hearing him read aloud from Isaiah, to approach the man. He shared the Lord with him as he traveled, and he baptized him when they came across a body of water. Then, Philip disappeared. (See Acts 8:26–39.)

From what we know through studies of church history, that man returned to his home country, led the leaders of his land to the Lord, and helped to establish one of the strongest centers for Christianity in the entire region at that time. His follow-up program was one designed entirely by the Holy Spirit revealing the truth of the Scriptures to his heart. The Ethiopian—or Coptic—church is one of the oldest bodies of faith in the world.

Remember that the Scriptures say this about the sharing of God's Word:

So shall My word be that goes forth from my mouth; it shall not return to Me void, but it shall accomplish what I please, and it shall prosper in the thing for which I sent it. (Isaiah 55:11)

That's true not only of the Word of the Lord spoken by a pastor, teacher, or evangelist, but also of any word of the Lord spoken by any believer, no matter how young he is in Christ.

Trust God to be true to His own Word. Trust God to accomplish in a person's life what He pleases.

A Hunger for God

I shared the gospel and prayed with a young college student whom a friend of mine had previously shared with and given a Bible to. Two weeks later, the student came back to my friend and said, "I've almost finished reading the Bible through. What should I read next?"

> **IF WE LEAD SOMEONE TO A PERSONAL RELATIONSHIP WITH THE LIVING GOD, HE IS FAITHFUL TO KEEP AND CARE FOR HIS OWN CHILDREN.**

It is rather puzzling how some new followers of Christ seem to just take off and grow in the Lord with very little outside encouragement or nurturing, while others have all the advantages and resources, as well as support from family and friends, but they vacillate, backslide, and live in defeat with very little fruit in their lives.

That's an area where we just have to trust the Lord. But we can have confidence that if we lead a person to a genuine encounter with Christ and a personal relationship with the living God, He is faithful to keep and care for His own children.

Don't be discouraged when you see people fall away. Just do all you can do, with the leading of the Holy Spirit, in terms of prayer and discipleship; but realize that each individual is responsible to God and that God will continue His work in the lives of His children.

Questions for Reflection and/or Discussion

1. What does being a fruitful follower of Christ look like?
2. What is the key element to being a fruitful, reproducing follower of Christ?
3. Discuss the role of the Holy Spirit in relation to follow-up in the lives of those with whom you share.
4. In what ways can you offer a new believer follow-up support?
5. Who is ultimately responsible for a person's spiritual growth?

—14—

STORYING THE GOOD NEWS: THE "ORALITY" PHENOMENON

"How would you like to hear a story that will help you discover the path to God?"

This is just one of the questions you can use to introduce telling a Bible story that can result in someone responding to the gospel for the first time or experiencing a new spiritual awareness in his life. Questions such as this are "door openers," ways of engaging people in conversation, that lead to sharing the gospel. They are similar to the questions we looked at earlier in this book that help pave the way for you to discuss spiritual matters with others, such as "Have you noticed any signs of spiritual awakening in your part of the country?" or "Have you been thinking more about God lately?" Yet these questions are specifically designed to be part of a prologue to using a particular Bible story as a means of evangelism and spiritual encouragement.

One man learned and used this method of storytelling in a community in Southern Mexico, using an interpreter. After using an opening question and then offering some preliminary comments, he told the story of the Woman at the Well to five workers who were constructing a "spring box," which is a protected spring that serves as the equivalent of a well. One of the workers was a believer, but the other four were not.

After finishing the story, the man asked the workers a few questions, such as "What do you think Jesus meant by 'living water'?" Then, he asked if they thought Jesus still gives this living water today and if they'd be interested in receiving it. After hearing further explanation of the gospel, the four men who were not believers all expressed their faith in Christ right then. I heard a report that, a few weeks later, thirteen families in that community had come to Christ as a result of the story being retold by those workers. All through the storytelling evangelism of a man who visited their work site.

Spreading the Gospel through "Orality"

In most countries—both in those that are designated as "literate" and those that are considered "illiterate"—many people respond best to information conveyed through some form of storytelling. Seventy percent of the world's population (roughly four *billion* people) are nonliterate, oral learners or prefer to learn through oral means. They are known as "oral preference learners" or "oral communicators"—"those who can't, don't, or won't learn" through the written word or who learn best by nonliterate styles of communication.[1] This worldwide trend is known as *orality.*

SEVENTY PERCENT OF THE WORLD'S POPULATION (ROUGHLY FOUR *BILLION* PEOPLE) ARE NONLITERATE, ORAL LEARNERS OR PREFER TO LEARN THROUGH ORAL MEANS.

The term *orality* has been defined in the following ways:

The use of speech, rather than writing, as a means of communication, especially in communities where the tools of literacy are unfamiliar to the majority of the population.[2]

A reliance on spoken, rather than written, language for communication.[3]

An "oral learner" or "oral communicator" has been defined as a person having one or more of these characteristics…

1. Someone who cannot read or write.

2. Someone whose most effective communication and learning format, style, or method is in accordance with oral formats, as contrasted to literate formats.

3. Someone who prefers to learn or process information by oral rather than written means. (These are literate people whose preferred communication style is oral rather than literate, even though they can read.)[4]

Orality Methods Are Needed in the Western World, Too

Orality is relevant not only for reaching oral learners on the mission fields of Asia, Africa, and Latin America, but also in more literate cultures in the Western world, such as America.

According to oralitystrategies.com, a prominent organization that has embraced these concepts,

> Even in the U.S., Canada, Great Britain, and Germany, almost half of adults have "below basic" or "basic" literary skills. This is so even though those countries have claimed literacy rates of over 95%.[5]

According to the International Orality Network, 58 percent of the U.S. adult population never read another book after they graduate from high school, and 42 percent of U.S. college and university graduates never read another book after earning their degrees.[6] I find those pretty amazing statistics. They emphasize the crucial need for reaching oral preference learners.

There will always be a place for learning and revelation through the written word, especially the written Word of God. Yet, if we desire to *reach* the majority of people with the most important message they'll ever encounter, so that they can discover and begin to apply God's Word in their lives, we need to be able to communicate it in a way they can receive it—and that is most often through *hearing*, which may be combined with a visual presentation.

Does that concept sound familiar? As Paul wrote,

> *How then shall they call on Him in whom they have not believed? And how shall they believe in Him of whom they have not heard? And how shall they hear without a preacher? And how shall they*

preach unless they are sent? As it is written: "How beautiful are the feet of those who preach the gospel of peace, who bring glad tidings of good things!" But they have not all obeyed the gospel. For Isaiah says, "Lord, who has believed our report?" So then faith comes by hearing, and hearing by the word of God. (Romans 10:14–17)

Reaching and Discipling Oral Learners

As we have seen, some of those who are best reached through oral and also visual means are unable to read or write. Others just prefer to communicate orally and visually. Some people groups don't have written languages, some don't have translations of the Scriptures in their native tongues, and some may have part or all of the Scriptures in their languages but are unable to read the Bible with comprehension.

Yet the church's primary means of communicating the gospel for some time now has been through written forms. "Ironically, an estimated 90% of the world's Christian workers present the gospel using literate—not oral—communication styles. In order to reach and disciple oral learners, we must learn to use the strategies that are familiar and relevant to them."[7]

If we are serious about taking the good news of Jesus Christ *"to the ends of the earth"* (Acts 13:47) and making *"disciples of all the nations"* [more literally, "people groups"] (Matthew 28:19), as He has called us to do, we must understand what methods or types of delivery are most effective in reaching them.

> THE GREATEST CHALLENGE OR OPPORTUNITY IN COMPLETING OUR LORD'S GREAT COMMISSION WILL BE IN REACHING THE NONLITERATE AND ORAL CULTURES OF THE WORLD THROUGH *STORIES* AND *QUESTIONS*.

Very likely, therefore, the greatest challenge or opportunity in completing our Lord's Great Commission will be in reaching the nonliterate and oral cultures of the world through *stories* and *questions*.

In this chapter and the next, I will show you step-by-step how you can use Bible "storying" as you interact with your family members, friends, colleagues, and acquaintances, as well as when you minister the gospel in other nations.

The exciting thing is that stories are universal—and, with certain ethnic awareness and adjustments, they are transferable to any nation, people, or culture in the world.

How Do You Respond to Stories?

Think about how you respond to stories. Are you more interested in a class, a sermon, or even a conversation when a story is told, whether for illustration, comic relief, or to allow you to process the information? The same is true for the majority of people.

Telling stories often engages people at a heart level in ways that preaching, lecturing, proclamation, or explanation do not. People tend to enter a story and identify with certain characters in it.

One Central American man who had been trained in sharing his faith through storying went to his family reunion and told his family members, "I've learned a new story I want to tell you." The group of about thirty-five people listened with great interest to one of the Bible stories he had learned, as well as the follow-up questions he had prepared. He also told Bible stories on a public bus, on which fifty to sixty people were riding, and the passengers applauded him!

A woman who is involved in ministry in that region used to share the gospel by taking her Bible to public parks and talking with people. After learning about storying and the orality approach, she learned Bible stories and then went to the parks and started conversations and just told these biblical stories from memory. She has noticed a much better response from people as she tells stories and asks questions than when she carried her Bible with her. Apparently, people were less intimidated and more receptive that way. The Holy Spirit is using her storytelling to open people up to spiritual conversations.

I believe that the growing awareness of, and response to, orality is evidence that God desires to bring a larger spiritual awakening in the world, as well as renewal and revival in the church. He wants to reach people through the power of His Spirit-inspired Word—spoken by one person to

GOD WANTS TO REACH PEOPLE THROUGH THE POWER OF HIS SPIRIT-INSPIRED WORD.

another or to a group—and He wants to use *you* in the course of your everyday life to do this.

Simplifying the Gospel Presentation

Some years ago, I came across a book by Herbert V. Klem entitled *Oral Communication of the Scripture: Insights from African Oral Art*.[8] That book prompted me to think, *How can the nonreading people of the world be reached and discipled?*

It was reading this book, doing some other research, and brainstorming with a few missions leaders in an informal task force that resulted in my coming up with the "Oral Discipleship" concept (the term *orality* wasn't being used yet) and my speaking on the subject in seminars and workshops at missions conferences during the 1980s.[9]

In relation to evangelizing and discipling oral learners, the task force raised questions such as these:

+ How much and what does a person need to know in order to enter a living relationship with the living Christ?

+ How much and what does a new follower of Jesus need to know in order to introduce and lead *others* to a relationship with the Lord?

We were conscious of the need to simplify and streamline the way we presented the gospel and made disciples, as well as the fact that there are timeless and biblical principles that will work anywhere at any time with anyone on the planet.

After much prayer, brainstorming, and discussion, we came up with five categories of truth from Scripture that people need to know:

1. Who the Creator is—the nature and character of God. For example, God is holy, just, righteous, merciful, faithful, and loving.

2. Who we are—the nature of the human race and humanity's need to be restored to a relationship with the Creator; the condition of a person "in Adam" (before conversion) and the condition of a person "in Christ" (after conversion).

3. Why we are—God's purpose for the human race, both in creation and in redemption, and the outworking of God's plan in our lives.

4. What we have—the provision of God to carry out His purpose, including the nature of salvation and what it means to be a partaker of the divine nature and to have Christ living in us.

5. How we live—the practical outworking of the indwelling life of Christ in the believer, including being led by the Spirit of God, abiding in Christ, trusting in God, and praying.[10]

Our thinking in those days was to use a variety of methods and strategies to communicate these truths in such a way that they could be reproduced over and over again. Also, the assumption was that we would *not* depend on resources such as print media, recording devices, or other technology.

Interestingly, when I spoke to groups on the subject of Oral Discipleship, there was a good deal of resistance to the idea that one could make disciples among those who can't read—even though that had been the case for hundreds of years after the founding of the church in the first century.

At the same time that I was teaching Oral Discipleship—and even earlier—other individuals and groups were developing and using Bible storying and other oral methods of evangelizing and making disciples. Many other streams of what is now called the Orality Movement came together over a number of years, resulting in the formation of the International Orality Network, to which a number of noted organizations now belong, such as Campus Crusade for Christ, Trans World Radio, Wycliffe Bible Translators, the International Mission Board of the Southern Baptist Convention, Youth With A Mission, the Lausanne Committee on World Evangelization, and many others, as well as my own organization, Living Water International.

There are several streams of the Orality Movement, including storying, parables, the use of village and biblical proverbs, drama, dance, song, visuals, and other technology. There are also several streams within each stream. For example, the storying stream includes several forms of Bible storying, such as contextual, chronological, relational, topical, thematic, and systematic. The technology stream includes many different audio and video devices, such as the Internet, iPods, cell phones, and various types of recordings.

> THE MOST UNIVERSALLY APPLICABLE OF ALL EVANGELISM METHODS IS TELLING THE STORIES OF JESUS AND INTERACTING WITH THE PEOPLE WHO ARE RECEIVING THE MESSAGE.

Yet the most transferable, or universally applicable, of all the methods is people-to-people—telling the stories of Jesus and interacting with the people who are receiving the message. Moreover, one of the most powerful and underestimated aspects of evangelism and disciple-making is *listening* to the people with whom we are sharing. Listening, in order to build relationships and connect with people, is a vital part of the oral method of sharing one's faith.

Our Storytelling Model—Jesus

Of course, the best model that we have in all of history for sharing the gospel is, obviously, the Lord Jesus Himself. When all is said and done regarding evangelism, disciple-making, and the Great Commission, we have no better example than He.

Had the printing press, telephone, radio and other audio devices, television, Internet, and other resources and technologies been available at the time when Jesus was on earth, the argument could be made that He would have used them all. But let's look at things the other way around: the methods and strategies that Jesus used so effectively in the first century will also work today—in your neighborhood, city, state, and country, and anywhere on earth.

In Jesus' day, more than 90 percent of the people were nonreaders. It was basically an oral culture. Our Lord used all types of stories, questions, and so forth to communicate spiritual truth to His hearers.

He told parables, such as the parables of the good Samaritan (see Luke 10:30–37) and the prodigal son (see Luke 15:11–32).

He used word pictures, such as *"It is easier for a camel to go through the eye of a needle than for a rich man to enter the kingdom of God"* (Mark 10:25).

He used analogies: *"No one, having put his hand to the plow, and looking back, is fit for the kingdom of God"* (Luke 9:62).

He also used intentional exaggeration and humor: *"And why do you look at the speck in your brother's eye, but do not consider the plank in your own eye?"* (Matthew 7:3).

It seems that many of us in the Western world have lost the awareness of the power of witnessing by simply telling stories and asking questions—even though we continually use stories and ask questions as we interact in our own relationships. When we consider how Jesus made disciples, we see that in addition to reading the Scriptures in the synagogue, He modeled the life and character of God, spent time building relationships and community, told stories and parables, and asked questions—and it was reproduced in His followers.

We must ask ourselves: Have we often made the Great Commission more complicated than God intended?

For the first fifteen hundred years of church history, the kingdom of God was advanced primarily by oral means. However, since the time of Gutenberg and the invention of the printing press, there has been a shift to more dependence on print-based and literate communication styles.

The advancement in education and the dissemination of information—especially the Bible—that the printing press has allowed has been wonderful and transformational. Yet, generally speaking, there also came to be a neglect of the use of oral means of communicating the gospel over the last five hundred years.

It's not a choice of whether to use print or oral means but of using *both* in the most appropriate and relevant manner, depending on your audience and the circumstances.

An Approach That Is Both Ancient and Fresh

The storying method helps us to relate to the "DNA" and culture of the first believers of the early church. Orality is an ancient approach that is fresh and alive today as we rediscover the most basic way for people to enter into a relationship with God and to communicate and learn and build community with one another.

Most followers of Christ in first-century Galilee did not sit down with a scroll of the Scriptures to have a "quiet time" or devotional time with God. They meditated on the words they heard in the synagogue and also daily, from house to house, in the marketplace, and from the elders in their communities, such as the repeated admonition from Deuteronomy 6:4: *"Hear, O Israel: The* LORD *our God, the* LORD *is one!"* They gathered with other believers, sharing their lives and stories with one another. Later, letters from Paul, Peter, or James were circulated and read aloud in individual homes and house churches. The followers of Jesus repeated to their family members and friends the stories of Jesus' life, death, and resurrection that they had heard from the apostles or those who had come to believe through their testimony.

The Holy Spirit Is the One Who Transforms Lives

As we rediscover the methods and strategies for making disciples from the life and teachings of Jesus and from the early church, we should always be aware that methods and strategies are merely vehicles that convey truth. As we have seen, only the Holy Spirit can touch hearts and change lives. As believers in Christ, we are vessels of His life and channels of His divine activity who produce lasting fruit. What He did then, He can do now, in and through every believer in union with Christ.

PEOPLE COMING TO CHRIST THROUGH STORYTELLING, CONVERSATIONS, AND QUESTIONS DEMONSTRATES OUR CREATIVE GOD AT WORK.

People coming to Christ through storytelling, conversations, and questions demonstrates our creative God at work. Orality isn't a magic formula. The results it brings are not attributed to the giftedness of the storytellers or the information or sharing itself, but the work of the Holy Spirit in drawing people to God through His spoken Word. We know that the Word of God is living and active and has great power. (See Hebrews 4:12 NIV.) Most definitely, the written Word has power, as well, but the spoken Word echoes the way God Himself worked in creation. God spoke— and suddenly there was light and life. (See, for example, Genesis 1:3.) The spoken Word also echoes the way Jesus ministered when He was on the earth. He spoke, and people were drawn to Him: "[Jesus] *said to* [Peter and

Andrew], *'Follow Me, and I will make you fishers of men.'* They immediately *left their nets and followed Him"* (Matthew 4:19–20).

Similarly, when we speak God's Word, people hear, and they come to Christ through the power of the Holy Spirit. Witnessing does not need to be complicated. *"Whoever calls on the name of the LORD shall be saved"* (Acts 2:21). It is the Holy Spirit, not the method, that ultimately brings results.

Five Key Bible Stories

In Living Water International's orality training workshops, we are using five key Bible stories to great effect, and I want to share them with you so that you can use them, too: The Woman at the Well, Jesus Calms the Storm, The Demon-Possessed Gerasene (or Gadarene, depending on the particular Bible translation), Nicodemus, and The Blind Beggar (Bartimaeus). I have provided a written sample of all five stories in the next chapter, as well as tips to help you learn and present them more easily. Earlier, I mentioned that there are different streams of Bible storying, and these stories fall under the category of "contextual" Bible storying. *Contextual* storying means that the storyteller provides the setting or gives the context for the stories before telling the story itself.

In addition to being a vehicle for sharing the gospel, the stories comprise a training method or an equipping strategy for making disciples because they serve as an introduction to foundational biblical theology. As the stories are told, they can be used to teach solid Bible knowledge, as well as personal application of the Scriptures to people's lives.

Story Criteria: Biblical, Understandable, Reproducible

Because of their importance in both communicating the heart of the gospel and making disciples, the criteria for all the stories we tell in sharing the gospel is that they be *clear* and *true to Scripture*. They must therefore be…

+ biblical

+ simple and understandable to the audience (taking into account the people's situation/culture)

- reproducible (easily remembered by yourself and others for retelling)

As we will discuss further, you don't have to memorize each story exactly word for word—rote memorization isn't effective in these circumstances. Neither do you necessarily include every part of a given story. However, you need to make sure the main biblical message is retained and is clear to your hearers.

When the right stories are told and the right questions are asked, the Holy Spirit begins to bring amazing revelation and insight to those who are hearing the story from God's Word—often for the first time.

"Pre-Crafted" Stories

The five stories presented in written form in the next chapter have been "pre-crafted" for use with oral learners. They are especially effective when an audience already has some familiarity with God and the Bible. Later, we will discuss what stories can be used with those who aren't familiar with the creator God or the Scriptures.

"PRE-CRAFTED" STORIES HAVE PROVEN TO BE EFFECTIVE FOR MANY TYPES OF PEOPLE, IN A VARIETY OF SITUATIONS, AND IN CULTURES THROUGHOUT THE WORLD.

Pre-crafted means that they have been prepared ahead of time with the audience in mind and have been "crafted," or slightly rewritten, for greatest clarity. Most important, they have been tested and proven to be transferrable and effective for many types of people, in a variety of situations, and in cultures throughout the world.

These core stories, taken together, provide a frame of reference to demonstrate to your hearers that God has power over nature, power over the spirit world, and power to forgive sin, transform lives, heal the sick, restore broken relationships, and much more. They provide a basic theology about God, human beings, the nature of the human condition, sin, evil in the world, redemption, salvation, and a variety of other themes that can be drawn from them.

Again, for all the stories, we stay as close to the original scriptural account as possible, and any modifications are only for clarity or flow. The point is that these are key stories that will especially help to introduce and clarify the gospel for your hearers. Here is a sample of one of the stories, the story of The Blind Beggar:

> As Jesus was going out from Jericho with His disciples and a large crowd of people, a blind beggar known as Bartimaeus was sitting by the road. Bartimaeus means "son of Timaeus." And when this blind beggar heard that Jesus of Nazareth was passing by, he began to cry out, "Jesus, Son of David, have mercy on me; help me!"
>
> Many of the people rebuked him and told him to be quiet, but he kept shouting out all the more, "Son of David, have mercy on me!" Jesus stopped and said, "Call him."
>
> And they called the blind man, saying to him, "Take courage, cheer up, on your feet! He is calling for you." Throwing off his outer garment, he jumped to his feet and came to Jesus.
>
> Jesus said to him, "What do you want Me to do for you?" And the blind man said to Him, "Master, I want to see!" And Jesus said to him, "Go your way; your faith has made you well." And immediately he received his sight and began following Jesus on the road.
>
> (See Mark 10:46–52 NASB. See also Luke 18:35–43; Matthew 20:29–34.)

How to Present the Stories

How do you most effectively present Bible stories, such as the above, to others in oral form?

Use Pre-Story Dialogue and Questions for Context

First, "bookend" your story by providing your hearers with pre-story and post-story information, dialogue, and questions. Depending on the story and your audience, you will sometimes need to give more explanation and dialogue before the story, while at other times, you will need to give more explanation and dialogue after the story. Make a clear distinction in your mind, and for your audience, between the story itself and the comments, discussion, and questions that come before and after it. In this way, you will allow the Word of God to speak for itself.

Recall that the five Bible stories presented in chapter 15 fall under the category of "contextual" stories, and it's important to consider the world-view and customs of the target audience. You want to make sure you provide the proper context, both biblically and culturally.

For example, pre-story dialogue for The Blind Beggar might include this brief background information: "This story takes place toward the end of Jesus' ministry and life here on earth. He was on His way to Jerusalem, where He was going to be crucified for the sins of the world."

Context brings meaning. So, the introductions and follow-up comments and questions provide a story framework for those who have little true biblical knowledge or only a general understanding of spiritual things. I have found that this approach works well in places such as Latin America and East Africa, where missionaries and others have already brought the gospel in some form in the past. It can also work well in the United States, where there is declining church attendance and low biblical literacy but a general, and sometimes surface, knowledge of Christianity. Many people know something about God, but storying will help lead them from that general knowledge to an understanding of how to enter into a personal relationship with Jesus Christ and a restored relationship with the heavenly Father. Under these circumstances, stories can get to the heart of the matter more quickly than a linear and more literate presentation of theological concepts would.

STORYING HELPS LEAD PEOPLE FROM A GENERAL KNOWLEDGE OF GOD TO AN UNDERSTANDING OF HOW TO ENTER INTO A PERSONAL RELATIONSHIP WITH JESUS CHRIST.

To illustrate, a friend and I greeted a couple seated at the table next to us in a coffee shop. We asked some general questions—where they were from and how they liked visiting in the city.

Those questions opened the door for an extensive conversation about the training we were conducting on making disciples of oral learners. As we talked, we were also able to share the story of The Woman at the Well.

Like most people, the two enjoyed hearing a good story. The apostle Paul said, *"Let your speech always be with grace, seasoned with salt"* (Colossians 4:6).

In the case of this couple, the Word of God, as spiritual "salt," was sprinkled in their hearts, and spiritual salt creates spiritual thirst, making people want to receive more.

The occasion didn't present itself to ask them to respond to the gospel, but, as we know, that's not always necessary. The important thing is to obey God and to make known the truth to all who will listen. The Holy Spirit will continue to work in the hearts of those with whom we share the stories of Jesus.

In the pre-story dialogue, you can also sometimes ask preliminary questions for feedback to help you identify barriers and gaps in people's biblical knowledge and see how to build bridges from the people's lives and cultures to the particular Bible story you are about to tell. You can then incorporate clarifying concepts into either the pre- or post-story parts of your interaction.

Then, just before you tell the story, make a statement that shows you are about to give an account from the Word of God. You might precede the story simply by saying, "This is a story from the Word of God," or "This is something that happened a long time ago. It's a true story. And here is the story from the Word of God."

Tell the Story without Any Other Commentary

While you're telling the story, it is extremely important to remember *not to present any commentary on it.* Just relate the biblical account (as it has been "pre-crafted" for the hearers' understanding). Let the Holy Spirit do the work in people's hearts through God's Word, rather than trying to do it yourself.

Conclude the story with a statement such as this: "That's the story from the Word of God." Again, in this way, you're making a clear distinction, for yourself and your hearers, between the story from God's Word and the post-story dialogue and questions that follow.

Use Follow-up Questions and Dialogue

Follow-up or post-story questions and dialogue fall under three general categories:

1. What do we observe in this story?

2. What does this story mean?

3. How does this story apply to our lives?

Questions relating to these areas can take many forms of expression. I have provided a number of sample follow-up questions for each Bible story in the next chapter. However, as you become more familiar with the stories and more comfortable with the storying process, you will naturally develop additional questions based on your own insights and experiences, and based on the context of your hearers' lives, as the Holy Spirit directs you. These questions will bring out the truth of what you want people to understand.

For instance, after telling the story of The Blind Beggar, you might ask, "What was the blind beggar's life like before he encountered Jesus? What opportunities do you think he would have had?" or "What do we learn from this story about God's attitude toward the down-and-out or outcasts of society?"

In another example, after telling the story of The Woman at the Well from John 4, you could ask, "Why did the woman leave her waterpot at the well after specifically going there to get water?" There's a valuable message in the fact that she left it. People may respond with statements such as, "Because, after meeting Jesus, spiritual life became more important to her than even her physical needs." Other follow-up questions to this story might be, "Why did the woman think it was unusual for a Jew to talk to a Samaritan?" "What was the woman's life like before she met Jesus?" "Do you notice a change in her attitude as the story goes on?" and "Have you experienced a similar transformation in your life?"

Post-story time enables you to ask specific questions and to generate discussion that will help people to understand the Bible story better, see the truths and message of the story from the Word of God, and draw insights and spiritual conclusions from it. It also gives you an opportunity to provide more specific details about the gospel—Jesus' life, death, resurrection, ascension, and future return. You can tell people about God's plan of salvation and how to enter into it.

The people's responses to your questions and comments will help you to know what areas of their knowledge and understanding need clarification and will allow you to address critical issues and provide explanation. Always clarify erroneous ideas with patience and with respect for your hearers.

"What If I'm Not a Natural Storyteller?"

Some people don't feel they are very good at telling stories and therefore wouldn't be able to use this method of sharing the gospel. They hear others who are polished and dramatic storytellers, and they get the idea, *They're so talented—I could never do that.*

You don't have to worry about being a great storyteller, because you have great stories to tell! It's best not to focus on telling the stories with perfection and polish. You can adapt the storytelling approach to who you are, whether you have an outgoing personality, a quiet one, or somewhere in between. Focus on the stories themselves; get excited about them and the truths they convey, and you will become eager to share them with others. People frequently tell me, in effect, "I was never comfortable witnessing, but I can do this—I can tell stories."

> YOU CAN ADAPT THE STORYTELLING APPROACH TO WHO YOU ARE, WHETHER YOU HAVE AN OUTGOING PERSONALITY, A QUIET ONE, OR SOMEWHERE IN BETWEEN.

The main thing is just to get started telling the stories. You can begin with a person or a group of people you feel most comfortable with. Of course, the better you learn the stories and the more often you tell them, the more you will increase your effectiveness in presenting them and in emphasizing certain aspects and themes. As you practice the stories and begin to use them, you'll find yourself filled with ideas about places and situations in which you can use storytelling to share the gospel.

Always remember that the key element is the work of the Holy Spirit. It's not your transference of information or your ability to communicate but His power that makes the difference. As you share God's Word, the Holy Spirit will be speaking to people's hearts and changing their lives. (See 1 Corinthians 3:6–7.)

"Historic" and "Transformational"

Some of those whom we've trained in the storying and orality strategies around the world have used these words to describe their experiences with it and their feelings about it: "historic," "transformational," "...revolutionized the way I witness and share my faith," "It will change our nation," "It will bring revival." As you practice Bible storying yourself, you will begin to see its remarkable promise, as well.

A wonderful quality of storying (and other orality methods) is that it has multiple applications in multiple circumstances. For example...

+ Storying can be done by believers of all ages—adults, teens, and children alike. One man said, "Orality levels the playing ground so everyone can participate." His training group was amazed when a nine-year-old girl stood up and told the story of The Demon-Possessed Gerasene perfectly.

+ People at every level of biblical knowledge or maturity can be trained and mobilized for storying. If nine-year-olds and illiterate adults can repeat the stories, then every follower of Jesus can do this. You can teach people a story and have them practice it a number of times, and then they can immediately go out and implement the storytelling method. It is God's plan that we *all* be His witnesses.

+ Storying can be used in a variety of settings: at family gatherings, with groups of children, with teens, with adults, with senior citizens, with church groups, with clubs and associations, with friends and colleagues, in street evangelism, in prison ministry, in cross-cultural ministry in your own city, in short-term missions trips, in long-term missions work...the applications are endless. One missions leader in an East African country said, "We have tried everything we know to do to reach and disciple people. Now we know this orality method is the key for our country." The simplicity and reproducibility of stories make them transferable to a variety of cultures and even languages. If a person who is bilingual or trilingual learns it in one language, he can immediately tell it in another language. The stories are then passed along to more and more people.

The Benefits of Orality Training

You can also use the five pre-crafted biblical stories to teach other believers scriptural principles about witnessing, evangelism, and discipleship and to increase their understanding of spiritual truths so they can pass them along to others.

> YOU CAN USE THE FIVE PRE-CRAFTED BIBLICAL STORIES TO TEACH OTHER BELIEVERS SCRIPTURAL PRINCIPLES ABOUT WITNESSING, EVANGELISM, AND DISCIPLESHIP.

For example, after telling the story of The Woman at the Well, the storyteller can ask, "What do we learn about Jesus' witnessing methods from this story?" (The discussion can bring out the fact that Jesus did not lecture or judge the woman but found common ground from which to enter into a discussion that would lead to spiritual revelation.) Or, "What do we learn about witnessing from the woman's response to her encounter with Jesus?" (You can discuss the fact that a person doesn't have to have been a follower of Jesus for a long time to be able to witness to what God has done in his life. The woman at the well didn't need extensive training in evangelism first. She told her testimony right away to the other Samaritans in her town, and they, also, came to believe in Jesus.)

Similar questions could be asked in conjunction with the story of The Demon-Possessed Gerasene (Gadarene) from Mark 5, such as, "What do we learn about witnessing from this encounter?" (Jesus told the man to go home and tell others how the Lord had had mercy on him. He did so right away, and everyone was amazed. He didn't need any more knowledge at that point than his own experience of how Jesus had delivered him.) There is a common theme between the stories of The Woman at the Well and The Demon-Possessed Gerasene—we are to tell others of the mercy God has extended to us.

What is often so amazing to many well-educated and biblically literate church people is the new understanding that comes when they hear and learn these stories for the purpose of telling them in storying form. Often, passages of Scripture that they have read many times take on deeper meaning and provide fresh revelation. A pastor of a large church remarked after having received this orality training, "I've been a pastor for thirty-three years. I have read, studied, and preached on these stories, but I've gained insights that I never had before."

PASSAGES OF SCRIPTURE TAKE ON DEEPER MEANING AND PROVIDE FRESH REVELATION.

In addition, you may find that as believers hear the stories—and not just read them—the biblical truths will come alive to them, and they will respond in faith. For instance, one woman in Honduras attended an orality training workshop and learned the story of The Blind Beggar. She herself was essentially legally blind in one eye and had had eye problems for some time. That evening, after the training, she went home, closed her eyes, and prayed, "Lord, I believe; Lord, I believe." Then, she opened her eyes, and she was healed—her sight was totally restored!

So, storying is transforming not only the lives of nonbelievers but the lives of believers, as well. Stories and questions are becoming the vehicle for a greater understanding of faith, more open communication about it, and a concrete way of passing along biblical truth to others.

In addition, when you teach biblical stories to new believers who are less familiar with the Bible, asking questions before and after the stories often brings to light what people really understand about scriptural truth and what important truths they are still lacking. It provides an opportunity to discover error or false doctrine and to correct it.

For example, in a West African country, the story of Nicodemus was told, and a discussion followed about Jesus saying, *"Unless one is born of water and the Spirit, he cannot enter the kingdom of God"* (John 3:5).

Out of that discussion came the discovery that this whole region in that country believed that a person is born again only when he is baptized in water. While baptism is a vital part of Christian faith, the storyteller-facilitator was able to bring clarification to that village—that water baptism is the outward expression of an internal, spiritual new birth, and that one must believe in one's heart and confess the Lord Jesus in order to be saved. (See Romans 10:9.)

Sometimes, questions and dialogue related to storytelling can also uncover "syncretism"—the mixture of local religious belief systems with Christianity—among people who have had some contact with the gospel. When syncretism is uncovered, the distinctions between the local religious beliefs and biblical truth can be clearly presented.

Other Storying Methods

So far, I have been describing what I call a contextual Bible storying approach. These are stories and questions that are developed ahead of time for audiences that have at least some concept of the creator God, Jesus as the Son of God, and Christianity. But what about people who have little or no concept of God the Father and the deity of Jesus? This would include many from Islamic nations, certain Asian regions, and parts of Africa, which have been largely unreached with the gospel and have not been exposed to the New Testament and biblical Christianity. Another example would be people from a country whose government is atheistic and has imposed atheism on its citizens for many years. Many people from nations and regions such as I've described above do not usually have access to Bibles and Christian literature, and even if they did, their lives would be in danger if they were to be caught using them; so Bible storying may be an especially effective way of reaching them, spreading the gospel person-to-person, and supporting house churches.

In these circumstances, other orality strategies or storying methods may be more appropriate and effective. These settings involve different contexts, and therefore different stories should be used. This is where we especially need to consider the worldview and customs of the receptor culture.

Rather than using the five stories we have discussed, which highlight key biblical truths, you could use chronological Bible storying, for example, which starts at the beginning and builds up to God's plan of redemption and Christ's sacrifice on the cross for our sins. It covers such essential topics as the eternal God, the creation of the spirit world, the creation of the earth, the creation of Adam and Eve, the fall of humanity, the promise of a Redeemer, Cain and Abel, the outworking of God's plan through His people, and the life, ministry, death, and resurrection of Jesus Christ.

> **EFFECTIVE BIBLE STORYING REQUIRES YOU TO BE A GOOD LISTENER FIRST AND A STORYTELLER SECOND.**

Effective Bible storying requires you to be a good listener first and a storyteller second. You listen to the people as they describe themselves and their lives. You take into account their worldviews and cultures. You hear and learn, and you share aspects of your own personal life, before engaging in any direct evangelism. This includes what is called "relational" storying—giving your own personal testimony of salvation and how you've been transformed by coming to know Jesus and by having an ongoing relationship with Him, and also describing other ways in which God has worked in your life. While listening to your audience, listen to the Holy Spirit, also, and follow His leading.

Then, craft and present various biblical stories that are especially relevant and understandable to your audience. For your pre-story dialogue, you might expand on the question I used to begin this chapter, "How would you like to hear a story that will help you discover the path to God?" and add, "Well, this is a true story that happened a long time ago...."

For example, in my hometown of Houston, Texas, refugees from Bhutan, a country south of China that has an atheistic and Buddhist background, are being introduced to the gospel through a ministry that is using stories, dialogue, and questions to reach them.

Presenting chronological Bible storying to unreached people groups is obviously somewhat more involved than using the five-story approach we've talked about. You have to spend more time building relationships, crafting specific stories, and doing systematic teaching.

Most likely, except for certain cross-cultural and missions experiences, many of those whom you will encounter in your daily life will have at least a general knowledge of God and Jesus. Yet it is important to be aware of the various storytelling approaches and their applications so that you can know better how to minister to those who have no real concept of God, the Bible, or the Christian faith.[11]

Once you know that a person has received some teaching from the Scriptures and has gained a degree of understanding about God and creation, you can use more topical or thematic stories to present additional truths about who God is and to address special needs or issues. For example, after telling the story of The Woman at the Well, you could ask, "What do we learn from this story about how people from different ethnic backgrounds frequently react to one another?" (They often don't associate with one another; they exclude one another; they are sometimes hostile toward one another.) "In contrast, what do we learn about what Jesus thinks of people of different backgrounds?" (He didn't separate Himself from the Samaritan woman but engaged her in an important conversation about spiritual truth.) "Why were the disciples amazed when they came back and saw that Jesus was talking with a woman?" (The social custom of the day was that men didn't talk to women publicly, especially women of her reputation.) "What is God's view of people?" (He is concerned with all people, regardless of their ethnic, racial, or personal backgrounds, because He created all people in His own image, He loves them, and He desires a restored relationship with them.)

Again, biblical storytelling is not just about the transfer of facts and information. One of the fringe benefits of expressing the gospel and biblical truth through storying and other orality methods is the ability to have meaningful interactions with others, build relationships, and create community around the message and stories of Scripture. Moreover, in countries throughout the world that rely on oral tradition, when people learn biblical stories, the collective memory of the community or village helps to preserve the integrity and accuracy of the stories from one generation to another.

A Jump-start Approach

Much like the one-on-one witnessing encounters with hotel staff and taxi drivers that I described earlier in the book, sharing the gospel through Bible storying does not always allow for specific follow-up with your hearers. Please do not let this aspect prevent you from using this remarkably effective outreach tool. Again, God is able to provide follow-up for those to whom you witness. Remember that Philip witnessed to the Ethiopian before he was whisked away by the Spirit on another assignment. (See Acts 8:26–39.) Philip didn't have an opportunity to do follow-up, but a strong church was built in the Ethiopian's land because of his own witness to what Jesus had done for him.

Although it is important for people to receive follow-up and discipleship resources, the storying method exposes people to the gospel who otherwise might never hear it. It jump-starts the process. If we have the opportunity, storying and other orality methods also allow us to tailor follow-up, discipling materials, and educational resources based on people's backgrounds and needs.

Great Power in the Simplicity and Reproducibility of Stories

THE HOLY SPIRIT IS USING STORIES ABOUT JESUS, ALONG WITH OUR OWN STORIES OF SPIRITUAL TRANSFORMATION THROUGH CHRIST, TO CHANGE LIVES.

I am seeing a positive response to Bible storytelling everywhere I go. Something unexplainable often happens when the Word of God and the stories of Jesus are told and discussed in groups or communities. There is great power and impact in the simplicity and reproducibility of telling stories. The Holy Spirit is using stories about Jesus, along with our own stories of spiritual transformation through Christ, to change lives.[12]

As I travel around the world doing storying and orality training workshops, a common result is that after the first day, even more people show up on the second day who want to hear the stories. It seems "too good to be true," too easy, even miraculous, some have said, that telling simple stories about Jesus and asking questions can have such profound impact. The fact is that the key ingredient is not in the methods of communication or in clever strategies, but the miraculous and supernatural activity of God when the right stories are told from His Word and the right questions are asked. The Holy Spirit seems to show up and touch the hearts and lives of people at a deep level.

Orality is still a movement in process. We continue to learn as we go. Yet, as I mentioned earlier, there is within the modern phenomenon of the Orality Movement an awareness that God is doing a new thing—which is really an "old" thing. That awareness is that the life, Spirit, and teachings of Jesus are still at work to transform lives anywhere and everywhere He is allowed to move through His people.

It seems as if we are on the crest of a wave of a special movement of God. Are you ready to be transformed and to help transform the lives of others? *"Faith comes by hearing, and hearing by the word of God"* (Romans 10:17).

Questions for Reflection and/or Discussion

1. Why was "orality" Jesus' primary means of communication when He lived and ministered on earth?

2. What are the main benefits of oral communication?

3. How did Jesus make disciples?

4. For what reasons is orality the primary mode of communication in the lives of many people in the world today?

5. What are the key ingredients that make orality transferable to anywhere in the world?

6. What are the five categories of truth from Scripture that all people need to know?

7. Why do storying and orality have such great impact? What are the benefits of using stories and questions, compared to sermons and lectures?

8. Discuss how stories and questions help to build relationships and community.

9. What is the importance of simplicity and reproducibility in making disciples?

10. In what ways might you begin to incorporate orality strategies in your witnessing and ministry?

—15—

FIVE SAMPLE BIBLE STORIES FOR SHARING THE GOSPEL AND MAKING DISCIPLES

The five core stories from the Bible presented in this chapter have been chosen and developed both for sharing the gospel and for making disciples of oral learners.

Taken together, they provide a simple but foundational theology about God and salvation. They reveal God's character, the human condition, and God's purpose, provision, and principles for living. When you think about it, everything in the Bible relates to these five areas. They are another way of saying who God is, who we are, why we are, what we have, and how we are to live.

I have reviewed, studied, and meditated on the scriptural texts of these stories using various Bible versions and translations, and I have crafted, with the help of others, each story by modifying the text slightly for clarity and flow, for the purposes of contextual Bible storying. What follows are essentially the standard versions that I use when sharing the gospel through storying and when training people in the basics of making disciples among oral preference learners.

Any reliable, reputable Bible version may be used as the foundational text for the biblical accounts that you may craft for storying the gospel. Yet, the best way to get the most understanding from the stories as you are learning them, and to make them simple for people to understand, is to read the biblical accounts in several different versions or translations so that you truly understand and can visualize them.

Every effort should be made to stay true to Scripture and to emphasize the heart of the messages. Again, it is vital that all orality methods for

> **EVERY EFFORT SHOULD BE MADE TO STAY TRUE TO SCRIPTURE AND TO EMPHASIZE THE HEART OF THE MESSAGES.**

sharing the gospel and for discipleship be biblical, understandable, and reproducible.

I've included some suggestions for pre-story background and dialogue, as well as post-story dialogue, including a list of follow-up questions. You don't have to use all these questions, and there are many other questions you might use. How many or which ones you choose to use will depend on the circumstances and your particular audience. As time goes on, you will be adding your own questions or modifying these, as you feel more comfortable telling the stories and as you interact with your audiences and learn their backgrounds and perspectives. Remember to keep your commentary and ideas about what the story means separate from the story itself. Also, always be flexible and open to the Holy Spirit's direction.

Any parentheses in the stories are from the original text of the Bible story from the Scriptures and were not added by me. The brackets, however, contain optional word choices or explanatory words and phrases that you may want to use when telling the stories, depending on the situation of your hearers and your own preferences.

Also, for your convenience, after each story, I've listed in parentheses the reference to where it may be found in the Bible, as well as the main Bible version on which it was based, even though it may have elements of other versions in it, as well. Cross-references to additional accounts of the story in other books of the Bible are also given, if applicable.

Following the five stories, I've included a few general questions tying all the stories together. You can use these questions to help people identify biblical themes that the stories have in common and to come to a better understanding about God and their relationships with Him.

At the conclusion of this chapter, I have included tips to help you learn the stories more easily and with greater understanding.

You may learn them in any order. However, I have placed the stories in this particular sequence for two reasons. First, it is the order in which I usually present and teach them in storying training sessions. Although the story of The Woman at the Well is the longest, it yields many spiritual insights, and once you have learned it, you'll find that the others can be learned even more quickly.

The stories are also in sequential order as they occurred in the life of Jesus. For example, in the biblical record, the story of The Demon-Possessed Gerasene occurs directly after Jesus Calms the Storm. The story of The Blind Beggar comes last in sequence since this story occurs at the end of Jesus' earthly ministry.

I have sometimes taught the stories in a different order for the purpose of bringing out various common themes. For example, the story of Nicodemus might be told after the story of The Woman at the Well in order to emphasize the nature of salvation and spiritual transformation.

Start with any story and discover the joy of sharing your faith and seeing how God honors His Word and the Holy Spirit touches hearts and changes lives.

Pre- and Post-Story Guidelines

+ Give only a brief introduction and/or ask just a few key questions before telling a story. You don't want to overload people with too much information at first. (In orality training sessions, it also usually works better to limit the questions to three or four in the beginning discussions.)

+ Always preface the story with a statement such as, "This is the story from the Word of God." (Note: You don't need to tell people the exact Bible reference, unless they ask. A general reference to the Word of God is usually sufficient because when you are dealing with an oral culture that is not familiar with the Bible, it probably won't be meaningful to them anyway, at least initially. The story itself will have greater impact on them than where it is found. You may include the reference in subsequent follow-up teaching and discipleship, however.)

+ Conclude the story by saying something like, "And that's the story from God's Word."

The Woman at the Well

Pre-Story Dialogue Suggestions:

As an introduction to this story, you might ask your hearers to describe the physical symptoms they experience when they are very thirsty. In areas of the world where drought or lack of clean water is an issue, you can discuss the effects of these problems before telling the story and bridging to the concept of living water versus physical water.

"This is the story from the Word of God…"

———

Jesus left the region of Judea to return to Galilee. Now, He had to go through Samaria, where Jacob's well is located. Jesus, being tired from the journey, sat down by the well to rest. It was about noon, the disciples had gone into town to buy food, and a Samaritan woman came to the well to draw water. Jesus said to the woman, "Will you give Me a drink?"

The Samaritan woman said to Him, "You are a Jew and I am a Samaritan and a woman. How can You ask me for a drink?" (The Jews do not associate or have anything to do with the Samaritans.)

Jesus answered her, "If you knew the gift of God and who it is that asks you for a drink, you would have asked Him and He would have given you living water."

The woman said, "Sir, You have nothing to draw with and the well is deep. Where can You get this living water?"

Jesus answered, "Everyone who drinks water from this well will be thirsty again, but whoever drinks the water I give will never thirst again, ever. Indeed, the water I give him will become within him a spring of water welling up to eternal life."

The woman said to him, "Sir, give me this water so that I won't get thirsty anymore and have to keep coming here to draw water."

Jesus told her, "Go, call your husband and come back."

"I have no husband," she replied.

Jesus said, "You are right when you say you have no husband. The fact is, you have had five husbands, and the man you are living with now is not your husband. What you have just said is quite true."

"Sir, I perceive that You are a prophet. Our fathers worshipped on this mountain, but you Jews claim that the place where we must worship is in Jerusalem," the woman said.

Jesus declared, "Believe Me, woman, a time is coming when you will worship the Father neither on this mountain nor in Jerusalem. For the time is coming and has now come when the true worshippers will worship the Father in spirit and truth, for they are the kind of worshippers the Father seeks. God is spirit, and His worshippers must worship in spirit and in truth."

The woman said, "I know that Messiah" (called Christ) "is coming. When He comes, He will explain everything to us."

Then Jesus declared, "I who speak to you am He."

About that time, His disciples returned from the town from buying food and were amazed and surprised to find Jesus talking with a woman. But no one asked, "What do You want?" or "Why are You talking with her?"

Just then, the woman left her waterpot and went back to the town and said to the people, "Come, see a man who told me everything I ever did. Could this be Christ [the Messiah]?" The people came out of the town and made their way toward Jesus. Many of the Samaritans from that town believed in Him because of the woman's testimony.

So when the Samaritans came to Him, they begged Him to stay with them, and He stayed two days. And because of His words many more became believers.

The people said to the woman, "We no longer believe just because of your testimony; now we have heard for ourselves, and we know that this man really is the Savior of the world."

(See John 4:3–42 NIV.)

Post-Story Dialogue Suggestions:

"And that's the story from God's Word."

This story gives you an opportunity to talk to your hearers about ethnic and racial differences and how God views them versus how human beings view them. You can mention that in first-century Palestine, a Jewish person would never have dared to share a water container with a Samaritan because the Jews saw them as half-breeds and outcasts, and they didn't have anything to do with them. In regions of your nation or areas in the world where there is a lot of racism or tribal conflict or ethnic issues, this is a great point to elaborate on once you've told the story and started to make applications. In addition, you might want to provide some clarifying information about the relationships between men and women in first-century Palestine and how unusual it was for a man to have spoken to a woman in a public place and asked her for water.

Again, there's a valuable message in the fact that the woman left her waterpot behind to go and tell of her encounter with Jesus. You can guide the discussion from physical water/physical life to "living water"/spiritual life, from physical thirst to spiritual thirst, and to which is ultimately more satisfying for our deepest need. You can talk about the woman's background and her spiritual transformation and ask your hearers if they have experienced spiritual transformation, also.

Sample Post-Story Questions:

1. From this story, what do we learn about the humanity of Jesus? What do we learn about His deity?

2. What do we learn about God's perspective on different racial, ethnic, or tribal groups?

3. What was this woman's life like before she met Jesus?

4. Why was the woman coming to the well to draw water in the middle of the day?

5. What did Jesus mean when He said, "If you knew the gift of God..."?

6. What was Jesus seeking to communicate to the woman by using the words *living water?*

7. Do you observe a change of attitude in this woman through the course of her conversation with Jesus? If so, what is it?

8. Why were the disciples amazed and surprised when they returned from buying food and saw Jesus talking with this woman?

9. What do we learn from the fact that the woman left her waterpot—when she had gone to the well specifically to get water—and went to her town to tell about her encounter with Jesus?

10. Does Jesus still offer this "living water" to people today?

11. What do we learn from this story about spiritual transformation?

12. Have you personally experienced the "living water" and spiritual transformation that this woman experienced? If not, would you like to?

Jesus Calms the Storm

Pre-Story Dialogue Suggestions:

Depending on the group, you may decide to go into more background detail to set up a given story. For example, before I tell the story of Jesus calming the storm, if time permits and it seems the appropriate thing to do, I often explain that Jesus had been teaching large crowds of people all day. He had told some analogies and parables about the kingdom of God. Another thing He had taught, through what we call the parable of the sower, was about seed, sowing, and soil. Jesus told His disciples that the seed symbolizes the Word of God, and the different kinds of soil represent the various conditions of people's hearts and how people respond in different ways to God's Word.

I also often mention that in the afternoon, Jesus had been teaching from a boat pushed back from the shore. Scholars believe He probably did this because the water provided amplification, and He was creating an amphitheater effect. It reinforces the fact that Jesus was speaking and teaching to a large group of people who needed to be able to hear Him. The story also reveals that Jesus was already in a boat when He said to His disciples, "Let us go to the other side of the lake," and that the disciples took Him across the Sea of Galilee in the very boat He had been teaching from.

After I give this background, I say, "It was in this context that the following took place. Here is the story from God's Word."

––––––––––

At the end of the day when evening came, Jesus said to His disciples, "Let us go over to the other side of the lake." Leaving the crowd behind, they took Him along, just as He was, in the boat. There were also other boats with Him. A furious storm came up; the wind and the waves were so strong that the boat was about to turn over.

Jesus was in the stern [the back of the boat], sleeping on a cushion. The disciples woke Him and cried out to Him, "Master, don't You care if we drown?"

Jesus got up, rebuked the wind, and said to the waves, "Quiet! Be still!" Then, the wind died down and it was completely calm.

Jesus said to His disciples, "Why are you so afraid? Where is your faith?"

The disciples were terrified and amazed and asked each other, "Who is this? Even the wind and the waves obey Him!"

(See Mark 4:35–41 NIV. See also Matthew 8:23–27; Luke 8:22–25.)

––––––––––

Post-Story Dialogue Suggestions:

"And that's the story from God's Word."

There are many angles from which you could discuss this story. For example, starting from the physical and going to the spiritual, you might begin by asking, "What do we learn from this story about God's power over nature?" and progress to questions such as "Have you experienced any storms—physical or emotional—in your life?" and "What have you learned from the storms of life you have experienced?"

You may also want to bring up some interesting details in the story. For instance, the Scriptures say, "There were also other boats with Him." It doesn't tell us why the other boats were there, but I've found that the question often arises among participants, "What about these other boats?" It creates a really interesting discussion, with additional questions such as "Did the other boats also experience the storm?" Various ideas are presented, and I've heard some plausible suggestions that seemed consistent with biblical teaching as to why the other boats might have been with Him. Telling and discussing the stories always helps to put the listeners in the shoes of the people experiencing the events.

Sample Post-Story Questions:

1. What do we learn from this story about God's power over nature?

2. What do we learn about Jesus (His humanity, His deity)?

3. What do we learn about the disciples from the question they asked Jesus: "Master, don't You care if we drown?" What do we learn about human nature?

4. Why was Jesus sleeping on a cushion in the stern of the boat? What do we learn from that?

5. Why were the disciples afraid? What did they do?

6. Have you experienced any storms—physical or emotional—in your life?

7. If so, what did you do? To whom did you go?

8. What main lessons did the disciples learn from this experience?

9. Do you think the disciples shared the story of their experience with others?

10. What have you learned from the storms of life you have gone through?

The Demon-Possessed Gerasene (Gadarene*)

*You can use either term, depending on which Bible translation you or your audience prefers.

Pre-Story Dialogue Suggestions:

Depending on the background or culture of your hearers and their familiarity with certain terms, you may want to use a different word than *tombs* in this story, such as *burial caves* or *cemetery*, to explain where this man with the evil spirit was living. At other times, you also may want to substitute different terms in stories, such as the option of *control* I've given in brackets as an alternative to *subdue* or *region* as an alternative to *area*, for your hearers' benefit.

It is helpful to tell or remind your hearers that the story of The Demon-Possessed Gerasene occurred directly after Jesus calmed the storm. You can mention the fact that Jesus and His disciples had just encountered the storm on the Sea of Galilee and were arriving on a shore on the opposite side of the lake.

I often ask people to think about what Jesus and the disciples might have been feeling at the start of this story. The previous day, they'd had long sessions of ministry; then, in the evening, they'd set out across the lake and endured a furious storm. The disciples, at least, probably hadn't had a very good night's sleep and were weary when they arrived in the region of the Gerasenes. You can ask the hearers to be thinking about how they would you feel if they had gone through all that and then, when they arrived on shore, the following occurred...

"This is the story from the Word of God."

———

Jesus and His disciples went across the Sea of Galilee to the region of the Gerasenes. When Jesus got out of the boat, a man with an evil spirit came from the tombs [burial caves or cemetery] to meet Him. This man lived in the tombs, and no one could bind him anymore, not even with a chain. For he had often been chained hand and foot, but he tore the chains apart and broke the irons on his feet. No one was strong enough to subdue [control] him. Night and day among the tombs and in the hills he would cry out and cut himself with stones.

When he saw Jesus from a distance, he ran and fell on his knees in front of Him. He shouted at the top of his voice, "What do you want with me, Jesus, Son of the Most High God? Swear to God that You won't torture me!" For Jesus had said to him, "Come out of this man, you evil spirit!"

Then Jesus asked him, "What is your name?"

He replied, "My name is Legion, for we are many." And he begged Jesus again and again not to send them out of the area [region].

A large herd of pigs was feeding on the nearby hillside. The demons begged Jesus, "Send us among the pigs; allow us to go into them." So Jesus gave them permission, and the evil spirits came out of the man and went into the pigs. The herd, about two thousand in number, immediately rushed down the steep bank into the lake and were drowned.

The herdsmen tending the pigs ran off and reported this in the town and countryside, and the people went out to see what had happened. When they came to Jesus, they saw the man who had been possessed by the legion of demons sitting there, fully dressed and in his right mind, and they were afraid. Those who had seen it told the people what had happened to the demon-possessed man—and told about the pigs as well. Then the people began to plead with Jesus to leave their region.

As Jesus was getting into the boat, the man who had been demon-possessed begged to go with Him. Jesus did not let him but said, "Go home to your family and tell them what great things the Lord has done for you, and how He has had mercy on you." So the man went away and began to tell in the Decapolis—ten cities closely situated and joined by an alliance—what great things the Lord had done for him and how He had had mercy on him. And all the people were amazed.

(See Mark 5:1–20 NIV. See also Luke 8:26–39; Matthew 8:28–34.)

———

Post-Story Dialogue Suggestions:

"And that's the story from God's Word."

You might start your post-story questions by following up on the pre-story instruction in which you asked your hearers to think about how they would feel if they had gone through a full but tiring day of ministry, encountered a life-threatening storm, gotten little sleep, and then saw a wild, demon-possessed man charging toward them. This should get the discussion going well.

I have found that this story of the demon-possessed Gerasene resonates with people, particularly those in countries where demon-possession is often more manifest. Yet people of all countries can relate—whether personally, from people they know, or from news accounts—to the self-destructive nature of this man. For example, you could follow this story with a question such as, "Have you ever met anyone who exhibits a destructive spirit—toward others or toward himself, or who is out of control?" or "Why do people hurt themselves?" You can emphasize that Jesus did not just dismiss the man as crazy but had compassion on him and delivered him. You could also discuss the difference between the man's mental state before and after Jesus delivered him.

Another important facet to this story I like to discuss with participants is that it illustrates a spiritual principle Jesus had just been teaching His disciples. Recall that before Jesus calmed the storm and came to the shore where the Gerasene was, He had been teaching a large crowd of people and telling them parables, such as the parable of the sower. This parable highlighted the different responses people have to the Word of God. You can make a bridge from this illustration to the different responses of people to Jesus after the incident with the Gerasene. The townspeople were scared, and they asked Him to leave; they didn't want anything to do with Him. Meanwhile, this formerly demon-possessed man wanted to go with Him. What a difference! Who would have guessed it? By His devotion to Jesus, the demoniac was shown to have good "soil" in his heart, but the "soil" of the townspeople's hearts was "by the wayside"; they were closed to Jesus' demonstration of salvation and deliverance, and the gospel message did not take root in them. You can ask your hearers, "What do you think the disciples learned from Jesus and this experience? What do you learn from this story about responding to Jesus?"

Many times, after Jesus gave a teaching, He would use an everyday example or situation as a learning opportunity so that His disciples could truly understand the truth He'd been conveying. In this way, the disciples were able to see what He had taught them worked out in reality, in actual experience, and in Jesus' life. Talking about Jesus' approach of creating learning opportunities for His followers often generates good discussion for storying participants and provides them with additional solid Bible teaching.

You might also ask the group, "Why did Jesus leave the crowd on one side of the Sea of Galilee to minister to this one man on the other side?" This question relates to the topic of ministry strategy. The "big crowd" is not always God's priority at a particular time. His priority might be just one person, and that one person might have a transforming effect on many others. In the case of the formerly demon-possessed man, it did—he essentially became an evangelist and a church planter as he went throughout the ten cities of the Decapolis telling his story. His experience shows us that small numbers and individuals can be important and are often the priority. The individual is very important to Jesus.

Sample Post-Story Questions:

1. Why was this man living in the tombs (burial caves, cemetery)?

2. What was this man's problem?

3. How did this man know that Jesus was the "Son of the Most High God"?

4. Why was he cutting himself with stones?

5. Have you ever known anyone like this man? Do you know people who have self-destructive spirits?

6. What do we learn from the fact that Jesus left the crowd on one side of the lake to minister to this one man?

7. What do we learn about God's power over the spirit world?

8. What is the significance of the man sitting at the feet of Jesus after he was delivered from the demons?

9. Why were the evil spirits afraid of being sent out of the region?

10. Is there a problem of demon-possession today?

11. Can Jesus deliver people from the power of evil spirits today?

Nicodemus

Pre-Story Dialogue Suggestions:

When I tell the story of Nicodemus, I often say something like the following: "This is a true story that happened a long time ago. It is very likely one of the most important stories—if not *the* most important story—in the Bible for many people. And it could be one of the most important stories that has ever been told."

I set it up that way, and then I say, "As I tell this story, be asking yourself why this story is so important.

"Here is the story from the Word of God."

———

Now there was a man of the Pharisees named Nicodemus, a member of the Jewish ruling council. He came to Jesus at night and said, "Rabbi, we know You are a teacher who has come from God. For no one could perform the miraculous signs You are doing unless God were with Him."

Jesus said, "I tell you the truth [I assure you], unless someone is born again, he cannot see the kingdom of God."

Nicodemus asked, "How can a man be born when he is old? Surely he cannot enter a second time into his mother's womb to be born!"

Jesus answered, "I tell you the truth [I assure you], unless a person is born of water and the Spirit, he cannot enter the kingdom of God. That which is born of the flesh is flesh, and that which is born of the Spirit is spirit. You should not be amazed or surprised when I say, 'You must be born again.' The wind blows wherever it pleases. You hear the sound of it, but you cannot tell where it comes from or where it is going. So it is with everyone born of the Spirit."

"How can this be?" Nicodemus asked.

Jesus said, "You are Israel's teacher, and you do not understand these things? I tell you the truth, we speak of what we know, and we testify to what we have seen, but still you people do not receive our testimony. I have spoken to you of earthly things and you do not believe; how then will you believe if I speak of heavenly things?

"For God so loved the people of the world that He gave His one and only Son, that whoever believes in Him shall not perish but have eternal life. For God did not send His Son into the world to judge or condemn the world, but that the world through Him might be saved."

(See John 3:1–17 NIV.)

———————

Post-Story Dialogue Suggestions:

"And that's the story from God's Word."

You can begin by asking your hearers if they were thinking about why this story is so important as they were listening to it and what their impressions of it are. This will open the discussion to issues of eternal life, the need for salvation, how we can come to understand spiritual realities, and God's relationship to and great love for the people of the world.

During this discussion, as you are sensitive to the Holy Spirit's leading, you can guide the questions from the general to the personal as you ask people if they have experienced the truth of the main message of this story, and how they know this.

Sample Post-Story Questions:

1. What was it that motivated Nicodemus to want to know more about Jesus?

2. Why did Nicodemus come to Jesus at night?

3. Why was Nicodemus having such a hard time understanding spiritual truth?

4. What does it take for a person to understand spiritual realities?

5. From this story, what do we understand about seeing and/ or entering the kingdom of God?

6. What was Jesus teaching about the Holy Spirit by using the wind as an analogy?

7. In speaking of the wind, what did Jesus mean when He said, "So it is with everyone born of the Spirit"?

8. What must a person do in order to have eternal life?

9. From this story, why did God send Jesus into the world?

10. What does it mean to be born again, or born of the Spirit, and to believe in Jesus?

11. What is the main message of this story?

12. How have you experienced the truth of the main message of this story?

13. Why is this one of the most important stories in the Bible?

The Blind Beggar

Pre-Story Dialogue Suggestions:

I often set this story up by saying, "This story takes place toward the end of Jesus' ministry and life here on earth. He was on His way to Jerusalem, where He was going to be crucified—He was going to die—He was going to sacrifice His life for the sins of the world.

"And this is the story from the Word of God."

———

As Jesus was going out from Jericho with His disciples and a large crowd of people, a blind beggar known as Bartimaeus was sitting by the road. Bartimaeus means "son of Timaeus." And when this blind beggar heard that Jesus of Nazareth was passing by, he began to cry out, "Jesus, Son of David, have mercy on me; help me!"

Many of the people rebuked him and told him to be quiet, but he kept shouting out all the more, "Son of David, have mercy on me!"

Jesus stopped and said, "Call him."

And they called the blind man, saying to him, "Take courage, cheer up, on your feet! He is calling for you." Throwing off his outer garment, he jumped to his feet and came to Jesus.

Jesus said to him, "What do you want Me to do for you?" And the blind man said to Him, "Master, I want to see!" And Jesus said to him, "Go your way; your faith has made you well." And immediately he received his sight and began following Jesus on the road.

> (See Mark 10:46–52 NIV. See also Luke 18:35–43;
> Matthew 20:29–34.)

Post-Story Dialogue Suggestions:

"And that's the story from God's Word."

In post-story discussion of The Blind Beggar, I often emphasize the fact that *Bartimaeus* means "son of Timaeus" by asking some questions, such as "What was this man's life like?" "What was it like to live as a beggar in that part of the world?" In many parts of the globe today, because of factors such as contaminated water, disease, poverty, and birth defects, parents don't name their children until they are a year or two old. They wait to see if the children are going to live, because the infant mortality rate is so high. I point out that the same mind-set may have applied in the case of the blind beggar, who is called "the son of Timaeus," although we don't know the details of his background. Sometimes, this term merely indicates a person's surname (for example, Jesus called Peter "*Simon Bar-Jonah*" in Matthew 16:17). However, the man apparently was called by only one name, and it designated his family identity, so he may never have received his own name due to his disability.

Therefore, after identifying the man as Bartimaeus, I generally refer to him from then on in the story only as "the blind beggar." Doing so helps to reinforce to audiences the fact that he didn't have many options, and this is why he was forced to be a beggar. This point would especially resonate with people in certain countries where it is common to see beggars in the marketplaces and other well-traversed areas.

You might also bring out the point that beggars have a certain identity and recognizable characteristics. For instance, they may wear certain kinds of clothes that others wouldn't. Someone from a Central American country told me in reference to his experience with beggars in his nation, "They have their 'uniform.'" Understanding this fact helps to bring out the meaning of the Scripture passage when it says that the blind beggar "cast his outer garment aside" before he leaped up and went to Jesus. This may have been symbolic of the fact that he was not only prepared to leave behind his old identity and his old life, but that he also wanted to remove any barriers in coming to Jesus.

I often discuss the physical and then move to the spiritual, which is what Jesus did in almost all of these stories. He did this with Nicodemus and with the woman at the well. To move to the spiritual, you can talk about spiritual blindness and what it takes for a person to receive spiritual sight. You might generate a discussion around the following questions: "Who can people go to for spiritual sight? How do they receive it? What happens when people receive spiritual sight? What did this blind man do when he received his physical sight?"

As you can see, even though this is a short story, it provides great teaching opportunities. There are many themes and questions you can tie in to it. For all the stories, I normally try to ask questions in such a way that people come up with the answers and insights themselves.

Sample Post-Story Questions:

1. Who was traveling with Jesus as He left Jericho on His way to Jerusalem?

2. What do you think the blind beggar's life was like before he encountered Jesus? What opportunities would he have had?

3. From this story, what do we know about the blind beggar's knowledge of Jesus? How do you think the man knew about Jesus? What made him believe that Jesus could do something about his situation?

4. What is the significance of the blind beggar calling out, "Jesus, Son of David, have mercy on me; help me!"? What did he mean by "Son of David," and why did he call to Jesus using this name?

5. The name *Bartimaeus* means "the son of Timaeus." What does that tell us about him and his identity?

6. Why were the people telling the blind man to be quiet? What does that tell us about their attitude toward beggars and outcasts?

7. What do we learn about God's attitude toward the down-and-out or outcasts of society?

8. What do we learn from the fact that the man threw off his garment, leaped up, and went to Jesus?

9. What did the man do after he received his sight?

10. What is the main spiritual truth we learn from this story?

11. Can we make a comparison between physical and spiritual blindness? If so, in what way?

12. How do we receive spiritual sight? Who can give sight to the spiritually blind today?

13. What do spiritually blind people do after they receive their spiritual sight?

Questions Related to All Five Stories

The following are broader questions you can ask and discuss regarding all five key biblical stories. These questions are effective for follow-up when talking with audiences you've had the opportunity to tell several stories to, as well as for thought and discussion questions with individuals and small groups who are training in Bible storying. The insights they generate are beneficial for new believers, mature believers, and seekers alike.

1. What do we learn from these stories about God, man (humanity), sin, evil, salvation, redemption, and spiritual transformation?

2. What is the main message in each story?

3. What are a few of the common themes in these stories?

4. What do we learn from these stories about being a disciple and following Jesus?

5. How would you define a disciple?

6. How did Jesus make disciples?

7. What do water and wind symbolize in these stories?

8. What is the most important truth you have learned from these stories?

9. How will your life change from what you have learned?

To conclude this chapter, I'd like to give you some helpful tips for learning and presenting the above Bible stories, as well as other biblical stories you may craft yourself. Then, I'll provide some guidelines for hosting your own orality training workshop.

Tips for Learning and Presenting Bible Stories

+   *Repeat the Stories to Yourself.* The repetition of reading the stories over and over to yourself will help you to learn them. Preferably, find a place where you can read the stories aloud so that you not only read the words on the page but also hear them spoken. You can do this while you're exercising on the treadmill, for example, or during your devotional time. Then, practice telling the story, as much as you can remember. Begin to practice telling it even before you get it "perfect." Most people are amazed at how much they can remember when they make the effort. You can also practice telling the stories to friends and/or family members during mealtimes or while you are driving in the car together.

+ *Don't worry about word-for-word memorization.* Learn the stories so that you can tell them, but don't try to memorize them perfectly. Keep in mind that the crafted stories are true to the biblical account but are not exactly word-for-word from a particular Scripture version. If your preference in communicating and learning is more literate than oral, then it's especially important that you review the stories not only in the above form, but also in several different versions or translations of the Bible. Some of these are the King James Version, the *New King James Version*, the *New International Version*, the *New American Standard Bible*, and the *Amplified Bible*. That way, you will be able to truly absorb the story and its meaning. In general, oral preference people catch on to spoken stories faster than literate people do. Therefore, the big challenge for literate learners is to learn the stories well enough to tell them so that oral learners can learn and retell them (remember: simplicity and reproducibility).

+ *Continue to review and reflect on the main messages of the stories.* Once you've learned the stories, continue to reflect on them. I often review the five Bible stories in my mind. For instance, if I have trouble falling asleep on a given night, I'll think through the stories as I'm lying in bed. It's a great way to meditate on the Scriptures. You often get new insights from the stories the more you think about them and their main messages.

+ *Visualize the biblical scenarios.* As you're learning the stories, try to visualize the *scenes* in your mind—the people, the situations, the settings—rather than visualizing the *words* on a page of the Bible. See them on your mental "movie screen." If you are a literate learner, visualizing the story rather than the words may take a little practice. However, by doing so, you will be thinking in the same ways as oral preference learners do. When they hear a story, they have a picture in their minds. For example, they will see a

Samaritan woman, a well, Jesus, and His disciples. They're much more visual. If you have a visual image of the story, it will be much easier for you to remember it and to tell it. And, it may also make the story come alive more for your hearers, as well.

+ *Listen to recordings of the stories.* It will be helpful for you to hear recordings of the stories. For example, the husband of my Spanish interpreter has been training in orality and accompanying the team on ministry trips. To help him learn the stories, he recorded himself reading them on an audio device and then played them back and listened to them on a regular basis. You can use any technology you choose: a digital recorder, an MP3 or iPod player, a laptop, and so forth. You can record all five stories and listen to them on your player as you take walks through your neighborhood, use the treadmill, drive around town or on trips in your car, do chores, and at other times.

+ *Focus on the story before adding gestures.* Some people remember seeing and hearing storytellers who use gestures, and so they try to immediately use motions while telling the stories. This can cause them to lose focus and sometimes miss conveying important elements of the narratives. My advice is not to think about these things too much at first but to concentrate on the story itself before incorporating any gestures. Just focus on learning the story and being able to retell it. Only when you feel comfortable with the message and flow of the story should you add other elements.

+ *Incorporate gestures and drama, as appropriate.* Various techniques and gestures can be effective elements in your storying presentation once you have learned the essential stories. Some of these elements include using meaningful pauses that highlight certain points of a story, emphasizing key words or phrases, using voice inflection, motioning with your fingers and hands, and so forth. For example, since I have been doing storying for some time, I can now tell a story in such a way that it will be obvious to the listener what the most important points of that story are, because I'll use emphasis, I'll use some gestures, and I'll use body language. Even using small gestures with your hands or fingers is helpful, such as holding up two fingers as you say, "Jesus stayed in this region for two more days," or holding up one of your hands and spreading your fingers as you say, "Jesus said to the woman at the well, 'It's true that you have no husband. In fact, you have had *five* husbands....'" Remember that some people are just naturally more physically expressive than others when they talk, and this is fine. For instance, the woman who works as my Spanish interpreter is much more dramatic than I am! This style works very well for her. Again, use your own personality in telling your story.

+ *Practice storying with others.* See if a family member, friend, or small group Bible study would be willing to work with you in engaging in this process of storying for sharing the gospel and making disciples. I am discovering that even literate people often learn a story better by hearing it told to them. We normally retain a story better by hearing it and interacting with people and having a conversation about it than we do by just sitting and reading it. Therefore, get together a group of two to five people who will commit to learning Bible stories together for evangelistic outreach and discipleship training. You might start off by reading the story to another member of your group and then having that person retell the story as much as he can remember it. If you have a group of more than two, have each person in turn tell as much of the story as he can, with the help of the others. Assure the participants that they don't have to remember everything all at once; the important thing is that they repeat what they do remember. When I'm telling or retelling stories and providing settings and background information during training sessions, I will often pause at key times, just to see if participants will fill in some of the story. Or, I will prompt people by saying, "And then what happened?" or "And then what did Jesus say?" Keep repeating the stories among yourselves, and the repetition and practice will enable you to become very familiar with them. Then, you can use several of the follow-up questions provided in this chapter to promote additional understanding and insights related to the stories. You can discuss what the main messages of the stories are and how they apply to your lives. As you progress through the stories, you can begin to make connections between them, using the questions relating to all five stories, such as "What are a few of the common themes in these stories?" and "What is the most important truth you have learned from these stories?" It is often helpful to move from general questions to ones that allow people to talk about their personal relationships with Jesus.

Guidelines for Hosting an Orality Training Workshop

After you have become familiar with the orality method and have learned the five stories in this chapter, you can lead a two-day orality training workshop to teach others the Bible storying approach to sharing the gospel and making disciples. The following is a description of what that workshop would look like and how you would lead it.

Start with a General Storying Session

First, gather all the participants together on the morning of the first day for a general session, whether there are twenty or two hundred people. After a brief introduction to Bible storying, tell them one of the stories. The Woman at the Well is always a good one to begin with. Second, retell the story. Third, have the participants retell it as a group, with different people filling in aspects of the story. You may want to ask for a volunteer to start it off, and you can prompt people as you go along using the same types of questions you used when practicing the stories with others, such as "And then what happened?" "And then what did He say?" "And what happened next?" These questions help to lead people through the entire story again. After they have heard the story about three times, discuss a little of the story's meaning by using some of the pre- and post-story dialogue ideas and questions in this chapter.

Break into Small Groups

Next, have the participants break into small groups—ideally of five people each. Depending on the number of people in the workshop and the circumstances, you might end up with four people in one group and six or seven in another, and that's fine. But I've found that having five people seems to work best.

After giving each small group a few sample questions to discuss after practicing the story, have everyone in the groups go around in a circle, taking turns telling as much as they can remember, with the help of the rest of the group. Make sure you reinforce the fact that people don't have to depend on their own memories but the corporate memory of the group. This will give them the confidence that they can practice the story and help each other out. People may not be able to remember the whole story at first, but with the repetition in the group as everyone tells the story, by the time the participants have finished that first small group exercise and have discussed the sample questions you've given them, everyone should know it fairly well.

Bring People Back into Another General Session

Then, bring everyone back together into one group for another general session. Ask a volunteer to retell the story before the whole group. By this time, everyone will have heard the story about nine or ten times.

Then, bring out the main message of the story by asking questions relating to the three general categories: "What do we observe?" "What does it mean?" and "How does it apply to our lives?" Depending on the size of the particular group, the time frame you are working with, and the group's particular interests, you may find yourself spending more time doing certain aspects of the training than others. That's all right. You tailor the workshop for the group, so there's a lot of leeway with this method.

Remember, you don't have to use all the prepared questions. Choose those you feel are most relevant to the group and the way the discussion is going. In addition, questions may come up that are not in the pre-crafted presentation. Be sensitive to the Holy Spirit's leading and to what He is doing in the lives of the participants.

The whole process of learning the story through the general and small-group sessions usually takes about an hour and a half, and then you can give everyone a short break before the next session.

Repeat the Storying Sessions

After the break, reconvene the large group and ask them, "Well, are you ready for the next story?" Then, go on to the next story, repeating the same process you used for the first one.

On the first day of the workshop, you will teach two stories in the morning and one in the afternoon. This means that three different times for three stories, you'll have the large group storytelling and review session, the small group storytelling and discussions, and the large group story review and application questions. On the second day, you'll teach the other two stories in the same way. As you add more stories, you can begin to ask the broader questions, such as "What are the common themes?" "What's the main message?" "What speaks to you?" "What's the most important thing in this story for you?" and "How does it apply to your life?"

Through these types of questions, you can get into in-depth discussions with the workshop participants. People begin to open up and share their experiences, so that you can then ask the deeper and more personal spiritual questions, like "How have you experienced Jesus' living water?" and "How have you experienced the new birth?"

I have found that the more people learn the stories, the more they become engaged in the storying process. Their energy levels go up because they're so excited and involved.

At the end of the first day, encourage people to make the effort to tell at least one of the stories to at least one other person that afternoon or evening.

Then, on the morning of the second day, you can provide an opportunity for people to give feedback. For example, you can ask them, "How many of you had an opportunity to tell a story to someone outside this workshop yesterday afternoon or last evening?" Often, some will say they did, and you can then inquire, "What stories did you tell?" and "What happened?" I've heard people report glowing testimonies during this part of the workshop, such as "I shared this story with someone, and that person received Christ." Testimonies such as these will energize your workshop participants for the second day's training.

If you follow these general guidelines, therefore, you will be able to host an exciting orality training workshop. As you do, keep the following several points in mind:

Stay Flexible

Don't try to be too structured or use a cookie-cutter approach or template to teaching the sessions. Have a general direction in which you're going, and then be open to the group and the experiences, backgrounds, and cultures of those participating. Every group is a little different, but there are similar patterns and responses to the biblical

REVIEW AND REPETITION ARE KEYS TO LEARNING.

storying method among all groups. One of the recurring themes is that review and repetition are keys to learning. The process gets people engaged. They learn the stories and begin to have some basic understanding of their themes and importance. Then, you build on that.

Encourage People to Enter the World of the Oral Learner

When we conduct the orality workshops, we tell the participants, "We want you to enter the world of the oral learner." We tell them that there's a learning experience we want them to engage in. People who are more educated and literate, such as pastors and Sunday school teachers, often want to pull their Bibles out and check out how the story compares to their Bible versions when they're hearing it. Yet they will learn the stories better and more easily if they're willing to listen and learn as an oral learner would.

Sometimes, I point out to people that much of the Bible and other classic literature was told orally for many, many years before it was written down. So, I don't even provide any specific Bible references for the stories at first but just say that the story is from the Word of God. I ask people to put away their Bibles, notes, cell phones, laptops, and any other technical or literate resources they may have and, for the duration of the training session, to listen as an oral learner would.

For some people who are just beginning the training, being told to put their Bibles away is almost a sacrilege, and they may wonder what kind of a workshop this is. So, you need to be able to explain the reason for it.

However, using the example of the Bereans from the book of Acts, I also encourage people that there will be a time *later* for them to search the Scriptures, to compare the crafted stories with them, and to use the Bible to help them learn the story better, to study it, and to reinforce it in their minds and lives through their own personal study.

> *Now the Bereans were of more noble character than the Thessalonians, for they received the message with great eagerness and examined the Scriptures every day to see if what Paul said was true.*
>
> (Acts 17:11 NIV)

This approach works very well. In fact, by the latter part of the first day, and on the second day, after the more educated and literate people have experienced the sessions, they usually have fully embraced the training strategy; they are engaged in it and understand why it is presented the way it is.

Moreover, you may find that sometimes you will tell stories in settings where some people have Bibles and can read and others don't and can't. Unless the people who have the Bibles put them away for the time being, they may communicate to those who don't have Bibles that they are at a disadvantage. So, putting away resource materials helps to put everyone on a level playing field.

Step In and Get Your Feet Wet!

The information on orality and storying from chapters 14 and 15 provides you with the guidelines and texts that will enable you to learn the

Bible storying method and also lead a workshop yourself if you want to. Let me encourage you that you will learn more by actually telling the stories than you will by just reading about them. If you have the initiative and are willing to step in and get your feet wet, you will discover how much you can learn, how the orality method works, and the joy of witnessing and discipling others through Bible storying. It will transform the way you think about communicating your faith.

BIBLE STORYING WILL TRANSFORM THE WAY YOU THINK ABOUT COMMUNICATING YOUR FAITH.

Conclusion

GOING, TRUSTING, EXPECTING

There is nothing more satisfying and fulfilling, no greater joy, than being instrumental in someone coming into a vital relationship with the living Christ, knowing that he is a brand-new creation in Him and that his eternal destiny has been changed.

I believe God places in our hearts a desire to know Him and to be a part of His redemptive activities in the world—advancing His kingdom.

It is a great adventure to be an instrument of His righteousness!

No "Plain Vanilla" Christianity

A friend of mine named Charles once said to me over dinner, "I'm tired of plain vanilla Christianity."

We were both in Washington, D.C., on business and had a good dinner together sharing about our jobs and our walks with the Lord. I prayed with Charles about his desire to see the power of God at work in a new way and assured him that the Lord would answer the desire of his heart.

We left the restaurant, and we decided to walk the few blocks back toward our hotel. As we waited to cross an intersection, Charles struck up a conversation with a man who was trying to restart his truck. It had broken down as he was making a turn and was blocking part of our crosswalk. He had diagnosed the problem and called his wife, who was on her way with a carburetor part he needed. We waited with him and began to share with him about the Lord Jesus.

"THE LORD MUST HAVE PUT YOU IN OUR PATH TONIGHT SO WE COULD TELL YOU ABOUT HIM," WE SAID.

"The Lord must have put you in our path tonight so we could tell you about Him," we said. "Both of us have received Jesus Christ into our lives, and it's the most encouraging thing that's ever happened to us. We no longer have to struggle with guilt over the things we know we have done wrong. We have a genuine peace and joy in our lives."

After sharing further about the death, burial, and resurrection of the Lord Jesus and God's desire to make him a new person, we asked the man if he would be willing to call on the Lord and receive Christ into his life.

The man said yes, and we were praying with him as his wife drove up with the needed part. Their teenage daughter was in the car with her. While the man began to repair his truck, we shared with his wife, "We've got great news for you! Your husband just received the Lord Jesus into his life. You need to do that, too, don't you?"

She said yes, as did the teenage daughter. Within a matter of ten or fifteen minutes from the time we came to that intersection, we were standing under the streetlight, our hands joined with those of this family in a circle of prayer. We prayed that their entire family would come to be united in Christ!

We continued toward our hotel and encountered a barefoot man, reeling under the influence of liquor and drugs. His jaw had been broken, and his teeth were wired together. He was muttering unintelligible syllables. We finally made out his demand for a cigarette. I thought of what Peter said to the blind man at the Beautiful Gate: *Silver and gold I do not have, but what I do have I give you* (Acts 3:6). Neither Charles nor I had a cigarette to give, and the third time the man asked, I looked him straight in the eye and declared with as much authority as I could muster, "I don't have any cigarettes, but I do have something you need. In the name of Jesus Christ—"

Before I could finish the sentence, the man began to cry out, "Oh, no!" He jerked into a stunned silence, as though something had hit him. I had no doubt it was the power of God. He put out his hands to brace himself against a wall behind him, and a softness began to come over his countenance. I continued to affirm the promises of God over him:

+ The Lord Jesus Christ is the King of Kings and the Lord of Lords.

+ The Lord Jesus Christ is taking power and authority over the power of the enemy that has been working within you.

+ The Lord Jesus Christ has freed you from the torment that has plagued your life.

+ The Lord Jesus Christ is available to you right now, and you can call upon His name.

As I spoke, he stood up, and his words became clear. He put on the shoes he had been carrying in his arms and tied the laces; then, we began to walk together.

By now, I had begun reciting the Twenty-third Psalm: "*The Lord is my shepherd; I shall not want….*'" When I got to the line, "*I will fear no evil,*" he joined in, "*I will fear no evil,*'" and kept repeating that line over and over.

"The Lord has released you," I assured him, "from the satanic stronghold that was keeping you in bondage. You can call upon His name now." The man repeated the name *Jesus* softly.

I could tell he needed rest. We hailed a cab and took him to a nearby shelter for a night's lodging. I went into the shelter with him, and Charles stayed in the cab, explaining to the driver—a Muslim from Iran—what had just happened to this man. Charles's face was radiant with joy when I returned. He had led this cab driver to the Lord. The driver said he had never seen such compassion and knew that the power of God in our lives was genuine.

THE DRIVER SAID HE HAD NEVER SEEN SUCH COMPASSION AND KNEW THAT THE POWER OF GOD IN OUR LIVES WAS GENUINE.

"Plain vanilla?" I asked Charles.

"No way!" Not for Charles. And certainly not for the truck driver and his family, the barefoot drunk, or the Iranian cab driver.

Need a lift in your spiritual life?

Share your faith with someone! Introduce others to the living Christ.

The Two Most Exciting Experiences in Human Existence

The two most exciting experiences in human existence are receiving Jesus Christ into your own life and leading others to receive Him.

If you haven't had that first experience, I invite you to do so today. Read Romans 10:9–10. Then, confess with your mouth the lordship of Christ in your life as you believe in your heart that God raised Him from the dead.

If you haven't led another person to Jesus Christ, I invite you to start sharing Him with others today through stories and questions.

Now is the time.

Don't miss out on sharing Christ with those whom God causes to cross your path today. They may never cross your path again.

A Word of Caution, a Word of Encouragement

At this point, let me bring a word of caution, as well as a word of encouragement.

A Word of Caution

> THERE IS A TEMPTATION TO JUST TALK ABOUT HOW GOD HAS USED YOU IN WITNESSING AND BECOME LAX IN DOING IT YOURSELF.

Once you have seen the Lord use you as a witness and in bringing others to Christ, there will always be temptations and distractions that can get you off track.

One of the major temptations is to just talk about how the Lord has worked, preach or teach about evangelism, and become lax in doing it yourself.

Years ago, I was interviewed on a television talk show on the subject of personal evangelism.

After the program concluded, the host (who leads a large worldwide ministry) told me that in the early days of his ministry, he had personally led many people to the Lord but had gotten away from it over the years.

This man was still involved in teaching, training, and producing resources (crusades, books, tapes, radio, TV, and so forth) but was no longer personally involved in evangelism.

Of course, all of those things are good. My point is that anytime we just teach, preach, and talk about ministry and get away from actually doing it personally, we really miss out on all God has for us. The Lord impressed upon me that I should make a major effort not to fall into the trap of just talking about ministry and outreach but to be diligent to practice what I preach and teach.

This is an area in which we all have to stay focused and trust the Lord to enable us to remain faithful. We can rationalize that teaching others is reproducing more witnesses for Christ, but there are always opportunities for us to be on the front lines, and that's where we should be.

If we are not personally doing what we are teaching others to do, our teaching will not be as effective as it should be.

A Word of Encouragement

As a word of encouragement, let me say that your prayer and devotional life greatly affects your ability to remain focused and faithful in sharing your life in Christ with others. It's our personal daily walks with God—walking in the Spirit and walking in faith—that will keep us on track.

When you sense that you may be getting stale or in a backslidden condition, ask the Lord to search your heart and to show you anything in your life that is hindering the Holy Spirit's work through you. Also, search the Scriptures, and seek God's direction.

As the Lord shows you areas where He wants you to confess and repent, claim 1 John 1:9 and receive His forgiveness and cleansing. But don't stop there—embrace the fullness of His life in you; take action and step out in faith in obedience to God.

Step Out in Faith to Initiate Conversations and Storytelling

Faith is acting upon the revealed Word of God. God has called us to an active faith, not a passive one. Remember that *"the just shall live by faith"* (Romans 1:17), *"whatever is not from faith is sin"* (Romans 14:23), and *"without faith it is impossible to please Him [God]"* (Hebrews 11:6).

We don't have to beg and plead with God to do in and through us what He desires to do and has promised in His Word to do. Our number one role is to trust and obey God.

> BE OPEN TO THE UNLIMITED AND CREATIVE ACTIVITY OF GOD THE HOLY SPIRIT THROUGH YOU.

Will you trust God for His grace and enabling as you step out in faith and initiate contacts and conversations, and as you begin to do Bible storying? Be open to the unlimited and creative activity of God the Holy Spirit through you.

Take that step of faith. As the late Stephen Olford used to say, "When we take, He undertakes. When we rest, He reveals. When we yield, He controls."

We really can rest in faith when we walk in faith. This doesn't mean that we are to rest *from* activity, but that we are to rest in His strength and wisdom *in the midst of* our activities. When we trust in His grace and enabling, it is His activity in us, anyway. So, we can rest in the reality of who He is in us and who we are in Him.

No Greater Joy!

God is looking for people just like you who will make themselves available to Him. You wouldn't be reading this book if you didn't have a heart for God and a desire to be used by Him.

Remember that *"the eyes of the LORD run to and fro throughout the whole earth, to show Himself strong on behalf of those whose heart is loyal to Him"* (2 Chronicles 16:9). Keeping our focus on God and His Word and continuing to trust, obey, and walk in Him (see Colossians 2:6) will enable us to continue to be effective witnesses.

There is no greater joy than knowing and experiencing God in all His fullness, being in the flow of His activity, and seeing others come into His kingdom.

Questions for Reflection and/or Discussion

1. Give some examples of how the Holy Spirit is unlimited in the ways He draws people to enter a relationship with Christ.

2. What is a major temptation that a person can experience after he's seen the Lord use him as a witness?

3. What will enable you to remain focused and faithful in sharing your life in Christ with others?

4. How can you show God's love to people today as you step out in faith and initiate contacts and conversations?

5. What is the greatest joy in a believer's life?

NOTES

Introduction

1. For more information on oral preference learners and the orality movement, see chapters 14 and 15 and organizations such as the International Orality Network, www.oralbible.com.

2. "O Questions & Answers: This is the 21st century and most people around the world read, right?" Orality Strategies, http://www.oralitystrategies.com/about_qa.cfm.

3. A. W. Tozer, *The Pursuit of God* (Camp Hill, PA: Wingspread Publishers, 2007), 62.

4. Charles Spurgeon, *The Soulwinner* (New Kensington, PA: Whitaker House, 1995), 189.

Chapter Four

1. Ralph D. Winter, Phil Bogosian, Larry Boggan, Frank Markow, and Wendell Hyde, "The Amazing Countdown Facts," U.S. Center for World Mission, http://www.uscwm.org/uploads/pdf/adoptapeople/amazingcountdown.pdf.

Chapter Six

1. "Survey Shows How Christians Share Their Faith," Barna Group, January 31, 2005, http://www.barna.org/barna-update/article/5-barna-update/186.

Chapter Ten

1. C. S. Lewis, *Mere Christianity* (New York: HarperOne [a division of HarperCollins Publishers], 2001), viii.

Chapter Fourteen

1. David Claydon, Series Editor, "Making Disciples of Oral Learners," Lausanne Occasional Paper No. 54, 2004 Forum for World Evangelization, Pattaya, Thailand, Lausanne Committee for World Evangelization and its National Committees around the world, 2005, http://www.lausanne.org/documents/2004forum/LOP54_IG25.pdf.

2. Richard Nordquist, "Orality," About.com Guide, http://grammar.about.com/od/mo/g/oralityterm.htm.

3. "Orality," http://www.yourdictionary.com/orality.

4. International Orality Network, http://www.oralbible.com/oral-learning.

5. "O Questions & Answers: This is the 21st century and most people around the world read, right?" Orality Strategies, http://www.oralitystrategies.com/about_qa.cfm.

6. Samuel Chiang and others, eds., *Making Disciples of Oral Learners* (Lima, NY: Elim Publishing and International Orality Network, 2005), 55.

7. "Contextual Bible Storying: An Orality Training Workshop," http://www.water.cc/storying. See also Samuel Chang and others, eds., *Making Disciples of Oral Learners*, 3.

8. Herbert V. Klem, *Oral Communication of the Scripture: Insights from African Oral Art* (Pasadena, CA: William Carey Library Publishers, 1981).

9. The Billy Graham Center Archives at Wheaton College contains, among other recordings, an audiotape of the "Oral Discipleship" workshop Jerry Wiles conducted at "Congress 88, That the World May Know." This conference was held in Chicago from August 4–7, 1988, and was attended by 15,000 Christian church leaders, who attended a number of large and smaller group sessions on evangelism and missions. http://www.wheaton.edu/bgc/archives/GUIDES/595.htm (see T145).

10. These ideas were included in a concept paper by Jerry Wiles, "Oral Discipleship: A Strategy of Evangelism and Discipleship Designed to Reach Primarily the Non-Reading People of the World, Using Oral (Verbal) Methods," 1983.

11. For more information on storying and other aspects of orality, as well as resources and materials, please refer to the International Orality Network, www.oralbible.com.

12. For more on this, see Samuel Chiang and others, eds., *Orality Breakouts: Using Heart Language to Transform Hearts*, Lausanne Committee for World Evangelization and International Orality Network, 2010. Jerry Wiles is mentioned in chapter 2, "Three CEOs Leading Change," and contributed to other portions of the book.

About the Author

Jerry N. Wiles has received worldwide recognition for his involvement in outreach strategy development, and his innovative and highly effective personal evangelism style has been acclaimed by a broad spectrum of church leaders. He is heard daily on the KHCB Radio Network and several other media outlets. His program *Winning Others to Christ* has been broadcast in 174 countries worldwide. He has also been a frequent guest on radio and television talk shows and has traveled extensively as a public speaker.

Wiles is president emeritus of Living Water International. Living Water is one of the world's leading faith-based water solutions organizations now working in Asia, Africa, and Central and South America. The organization exists to demonstrate the love of God by helping communities to acquire desperately needed clean water and experience "living water"—the gospel of Jesus Christ—which alone satisfies the deepest thirst.

Over the years, Wiles has served on the boards of several ministries and missions organizations. He has been a paradigm pioneer in the orality movement and presently serves on the advisory board of the International Orality Network.

In recent years, he has served with Houston Baptist University, Every Home for Christ, and Williams Baptist College. Prior to holding these positions, he served as president of Tennessee-based Bible Pathway Ministries. He was a regional coordinator for Mission America and the City Strategies Network of the AD2000 and Beyond Movement. He also served as national chairman of the Winning Way Coalition, a Washington, D.C.-based network of more than 200 Christian organizations, and as executive vice chairman of the International Bible Reading Association (sponsor of the 1990 International Year of the Bible). A former pastor and businessman, and a United States Air Force veteran, Wiles has traveled to more than fifty countries with his military and ministry activities.

Wiles earned an Associate in Arts degree from Williams Baptist College and a Bachelor of Science degree from Middle Tennessee State University. He did special studies in missions, evangelism, and biblical studies at Mid-America Baptist Theological Seminary and Southwestern Baptist Theological Seminary, and additional studies at Capernwray Bible School. He also holds an honorary Doctor of Divinity from Hindustan Bible College in Madras, India.

He and his wife, Sheila, have two grown children, Jonathan and Sarah Beth, and four grandchildren. His hobbies include karate, tennis, walking, reading, and family recreation.

For information on seminars, speaking engagements, or water solutions, contact:

Living Water International
P.O. Box 35496
Houston, Texas 77235-5496

Phone: 281.207.7800
Toll-free: 877.594.4426
Fax: 281.207.7845

Web: www.water.cc
E-mail: JerryWiles@water.cc or info@water.cc

Please note that all of the author's royalties from the sale of this book are donated directly to Living Water International.

10 Hours to Live
Brian Wills

I give him ten hours to live." That's what the doctor said after diagnosing twenty-two-year-old Brian Wills with one of the deadliest and fastest-growing cancers. Thus began Brian's life-threatening battle—both physical and spiritual—to receive a full recovery by focusing on God's powerful promises of healing. Through his incredible, true-life testimony of healing against all odds, find out how you can overcome the most hopeless of circumstances and discover joy in the midst of suffering. *10 Hours to Live* includes many other testimonies of people who have been supernaturally healed by the power of God.

ISBN: 978-1-60374-243-6 • Trade • 208 pages

WHITAKER
HOUSE

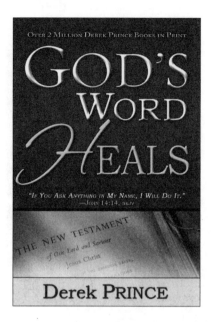

God's Word Heals
Derek Prince

From best-selling author and Bible teacher Derek Prince comes his most detailed teaching on God's miraculous gift of healing. Writing from decades of ministry experience, as well as his own miraculous healing, Prince explains how God heals. Through this incredible resource, you, too, can know the power of confessing God's Word as you get rid of spiritual obstacles to healing. Experience the miraculous provision of God that brings us out of death and into life! Lean on Him and stay plugged into the divine healing power of your heavenly Father.

ISBN: 978-1-60374-210-8 ✦ Trade ✦ 256 pages

WHITAKER
HOUSE